A NEW SUIT FOR LAZARUS

A NEW SUIT FOR LAZARUS

Joseph Battaglia

THOMAS NELSON PUBLISHERS
NASHVILLE

Published in Nashville, Tennessee, by Thomas Nelson, Inc., and distributed in Canada by Lawson Falle, Ltd., Cambridge, Ontario.

Scripture quotations are from The Holy Bible: NEW INTER-NATIONAL VERSION. Copyright © 1978 by the New York International Bible Society. Used by permission of Zondervan Bible Publishers.

Library of Congress Cataloging-in-Publication Data

Battaglia, Joseph.
    A new suit for Lazarus / Joseph Battaglia.
      p. cm.
    ISBN 0-8407-3182-5
    1. Christian life—1960-   I. Title
    BV4501.2.B3843   1991
    248.4—dc20   90-48861

Printed in the United States of America

1 2 3 4 5 6 7 — 96 95 94 93 92 91

*To my wife, LuAnn, and daughter, Alanna,
whom I consider living apologetics that
prove the existence of God!*

Contents

Part Three—A RENEWED MIND

"To be made new in the attitude of your minds"
(Eph. 4:23).

Prologue

In the eleventh chapter of John, one of the most unique events in history took place—the resurrection of Lazarus. A man dead for four days came back to life. Miraculous! At the time, Jesus was confronted with an impossible situation, or so the people around Him must have thought. But He said to them, "Did I not say to you that if you would believe, you would see the glory of God?" (John 11:40).

"He (Jesus) called in a loud voice, 'Lazarus, come out!' And he who had died came out bound hand and foot with graveclothes, and his face was wrapped with a cloth" (John 11:43–44). What a sight he must have been as he shuffled out of the tomb! I'm sure I can see it now: Pharisaical jaws dropping; Sadducees, who didn't believe in the resurrection, turning to each other and saying, "Don't confuse me with the facts"; bug-eyed people by the hundreds staring at a corpse no longer a corpse.

People still stand in awe as to the kind of people Jesus resurrects: modern-day Lazaruses like drug addicts and prostitutes, along with white collar criminals and blue collar workers, presidents and paupers, you and me. Each of us, like Lazarus, was bound up and entombed in our lifestyles of death until Jesus called us out and freed us not just from the appearance of death, but also from the stench of death. What a marvelous and total transformation!

"Jesus said to them, 'Loose him and let him go'" (John 11:44). Lazarus was alive! He was free! Given a new life, and a new look.

This passage is especially significant to everyone who's been raised to newness in Christ. All of us were dead like Lazarus. And when we are "resurrected from the dead" we, too, come limping out of the grave of our former lives into the waiting arms of previously resurrected people. The grave clothes that bind us are removed, and we are set free not just to follow Christ but, more appropriately, *to act as Christ*.

Immediately upon our resurrection, we are promised a lifestyle finely tailored and designed by the One who knows us best. Our lives take on a special significance, controlled and dominated by God's Spirit living within us. We're given new minds that think new thoughts, new characters that develop new relationships born out of love for others and not for ourselves, new insights with the ability to say no when everyone else around us says yes, and new power to conduct ourselves in such a way that others can see the results and shuffle out of their tombs too.

At times, though, instead of allowing Christ to tailor new saints with their newfound freedom and identity, we have a tendency to immediately outfit them with the things that we find comfortable to wear—our denominational peculiarities, traditions, or points of theology. Unfortunately, our clothes don't fit them, and you can tell. It's not hard to spot an uncomfortable Christian. We tell them, "You're now free to conform," and they become bound up once again.

My years of working at the grassroots level with Christians from all types of churches and parachurch groups and listening to conversations on Christian radio talk shows have convinced me that too many believers experience their faith vicariously or are simply unaware of the tremendous joy in discovering for themselves how to integrate their faith with every aspect of their lives.

The Christian life is one of freedom and expression, not of conformity. Jesus promised us a custom fit, not just something off the rack. It's not a hand-me-down expression of someone else's faith. Jesus never calls anyone back from the dead to keep them bound up. He calls them out to freedom, a unique identity, and a renewed mind.

Jesus wants to custom fit a new suit for Lazarus.

PART ONE

Freedom

"It is for freedom that Christ has set us free" (Gal. 5:1).

1

Maybe Morning, Maybe Noon, Maybe Evening, and...Maybe Not

Every now and then, when world events take a strange twist, a number of believers start talking about the Second Coming. It almost becomes a preoccupation. They spend more time looking for signs: The Iron Curtain has fallen, which will allow more openness toward the gospel; the Common Market is coming together in such a way so as to appear to fulfill prophecy. Can Armageddon be far behind? All this makes for great speculation. I mean, aren't we concerned about whether Jesus will return this year? Or is it next year?

At times people seem to just be interested in *when* Jesus will return. I know someone who's been talking about it for the last sixty years. (Frankly, he may not have much longer to say it!) Some people's entire focus is the Second Coming, instead of Christ's message to a dying world or a call to sharing a neighbor's need. Just the Second Coming.

Certainly, there are signs that the Second Coming is around the corner. But who knows the length of God's block? Should we be so preoccupied with this idea of a Second Coming that it overshadows the reason for the first coming—that we conform daily to the image of Christ.

We see the Second Coming like a script from some old western movie where the cavalry arrives in the nick of time, bugles blaring and rifles firing, to save us from the enemy. I can see it now: Jesus riding at the head of an angelic column to save the Christians who've rallied their wagons in a circle to ward off the oncoming attackers.

We want Jesus to come soon so we can go from hell on earth to heaven with Him. Isn't that a great reason to have Him return? So He can *save us* from *our* problems and pressures of living in the world.

As Christians, we don't need the Second Coming to save us from the power of sin and evil on earth. That's why Jesus left the Holy Spirit, to empower us to live a life honoring to God. Sure, things can be hard. But, Jesus didn't tell us to wait for the Second Coming in order to be rid of these problems that plague us. Instead He said, "In the world you will have tribulation; but be of good cheer, I have overcome the world" (John 16:33). These are His words to us.

We need to get closer to God, not have the Second Coming get closer to us. Ultimately, only the former will prepare us for life in this world. We need to deal with reality, which happens now, and not wait for the future hope which only inhibits us from working through current situations.

Jesus' promise that He is with me regardless of my situation brings real comfort; trusting that I will be rescued from my situation only brings uncertainty. That's why Jesus told us to occupy until He came back. He understood our desire to gravitate toward the miraculous. He's looking for current day saints, not for people who will forfeit the present for the future.

Let's use the Second Coming as a calling to build the kingdom of God in our Judeas and Samarias, regardless of the work involved or the forces we encounter. The promise of Christ's return should be incentive enough to follow through on His command to continue working, not waiting. God has placed each believer in a unique position as His witness wherever he or she is, for that is where God would like to build His kingdom. My Judea and Samaria are wherever I am—at work, at home, at play. And whatever situation I encounter, regardless of how good or bad, Jesus promises to be right there with me with His power to overcome. That's reality. That's the freedom He promises—the freedom to relax in His presence regardless of the circumstance—like Paul in a Roman cell or Peter in a Jerusalem jail.

Let's not squander our freedom by following a timetable with no schedule. Jesus needn't come to relieve us from that over which we already have victory. The first coming took care of that!

2

Cowbell School of Evangelism

Have you ever been to the Cowbell School of Evangelism where you learn the "roundup" method of witnessing? This method reminds me of those films where hunters in the jungle use noise-making instruments to drive animals to an area where other strategically placed hunters and trappers await them. Some of the animals will fall into the traps. Others will escape. But all are driven blindly by the confusion.

In this scenario, people are driven to the

gospel, not led. It's witnessing based on works, not love; contrived plans, not Spirit-led opportunity. The more one witnesses, and the louder, the greater the stand for Christ, you're told. People are seen as "those to be won," not those with whom to identify. We plan a rally or crusade to attract people, and proceed to set 'em up to "receive" Christ by delivering a message of guilt and condemnation, or by putting on a three ring circus that attracts people like a sideshow barker. If we can get enough people to be driven forward, we think, surely some of them will make decisions. Our efforts are based on odds and percentages, as if in games of chance.

This roundup method is a bit different from the biblical model of evangelism that likens our lives to shining lights. Jesus knew that people would be drawn to a light source, namely us, if they live in a dark world without His truth.

Have you ever been in complete darkness and heard a noise? Do you run toward that noise or away from it? There's something alarming about noise in darkness. It breeds confusion and fear. As you grope for the way out, every step is painfully slow as your foot feels every inch along the way, as if one misplaced step will cause you to fall headlong into some hole, or who knows what.

On the other hand, have you ever tried to make your way in a totally dark environment and suddenly seen a light? Your natural inclination is to move toward that light, right? It doesn't make a sound to be functional; its value lies in its quiet presence. Light dispels your fear, brings understanding, and quickens your pace toward the exit. What a relief to know where you're going!

Biblically based evangelism is just like that light in the darkness. People are naturally drawn to it. It does not attempt to reach people by driving them toward conversion traps, but instead allows the Holy Spirit to draw them on the basis of conviction and need (which usually results in a more solid conversion). A conversion based on fear and confusion usually creates a fearful and confused believer, unsure of God's love and His Word. A Spirit-led conversion brings understanding of one's need and a desire to change one's course.

Sure, it may be easier to beat the bushes, make a lot of noise, and get people running in one direction like a cattle stampede and hope, by sheer odds, that some will fall into the kingdom traps we've set. But freedom in Christ means that I don't attempt to ensnare people for the kingdom because that's a result of my effort. Being a light will bring people to me. Becoming a Christian is not to be trapped, but to be let go. The Christian who was netted by a trap will always feel like he's in a cage. The one who comes to Christ freely will feel like a centerfielder in old Yankee Stadium. What space to roam!

It's always harder to be involved in a person's life and risk the necessary time, energy, and love to relate biblical truth to that person's need. But it's so much more fulfilling. The end result will produce a solid believer, much like spending time with your child will produce a more secure adult. In our microwave world, quick and fast is great for frozen dinners and potatoes, but it doesn't work in relationships. Coming to Christ is coming into relationship, not just with Christ but with other believers.

People should know we're around because of the truth we stand for, not because of the noise we make. Remember, with all that noise, not only will people know we're around, but they'll know how to avoid us. People can run away from us as fast as they can toward us!

Yes, some people will always prefer the darkness. But for those who are looking for the light, let's not drive them off with our noise. If Jesus had wanted noisy witnesses, He would've said, "Let your cowbells ring."

So ask yourself about your light. Is it on? Or do you have a cowbell around your neck?

3

Gunfight at the Carnal Corral

If you're like me, you sometimes feel the Christian life is like a scene from an old western movie. You're the lawman, it's high noon, and the bad guys are gunnin' for you. Your job is to stand against them—alone if necessary. You know that these guys are tough desperados and that you're in for a fight. But you're pretty confident because you were told exactly what to do in this situation. And there are other people in the town who will stand with you. Or so you think.

As you wait for the gang to ride in, a lot

goes through your mind. It's a hot day and already some of your strength is sapped by the sun beating down on you. The town is deathly silent, the usual chatter and noisy children's play nowhere to be heard. It's gonna be okay, you tell yourself. You begin to think about your strategy and how you'll handle the situation.

So you strap on your guns and walk toward an ultimate showdown.

As you walk, the pressure mounts. You start to sweat. You stop in your tracks. Up ahead, right in front of you, you see it. The Carnal Corral.

Many lives are lost at the Carnal Corral, the place of spiritual confrontation between Satan and saint, and of conflicting desires to follow Christ. If Christ is preeminent in your life, you're prepared for the fight and you have the right weapons and battle plan. If not, you're outgunned and outnumbered.

The gunfighter and his henchmen are right in front of me, just waiting and looking as mean as anything. They're waiting for my reaction. "I'm on the right side. Show me to the lions," I think. "The badge will help me. When people see it, I'll get the respect I deserve. The bad guys will tremble because it's the badge that counts, the symbol of my authority. That's what gives me power."

Face to face with your foe, you say, "Throw down your guns. I arrest you in the name of Jesus." You fully expect him to comply because, after all, you have all authority under heaven and earth. And you've used the right words. People are supposed to listen. But strangely, that's not what happens.

Suddenly, a shot rings out and knocks me to the ground. Ambush! As I run for cover, I sense pain and bleeding from my arm. Fortunately, it's only a flesh wound. I realize that all those quotes didn't help. What went wrong? What a time to find out! The enemy isn't running scared at all. And to make matters worse, he's coming toward me, laughing all the time.

A gnawing feeling of loneliness and fear begins to overwhelm you when you realize that one thing *is* wrong. You were hired but never trained. You were sent out ill-equipped and misinformed, on-the-job training at its worst. You were given a badge as a symbol of your commitment and authority. And that's all. You never thought it would be like this. When you were hired you were told that life in the town is pretty simple and easy. Now, that's all about to end. The enemy is waiting for you, fully armed, and aware of your weaknesses.

Unfortunately, many of us face life's battles that way—spiritually unprepared and unarmed. We may have the right battle gear, but we've been so busy trying to look the part or prepare for the battle that we forgot to follow rule number one. *It's not our battle in the first place.*

That's right; it's not our fight! You and I can't stand up to the fight at the Carnal Corral. We weren't meant to. Only Jesus can do that. We've been so busy thinking that God needs *us* to fight the enemy that somehow we've forgotten that it is the Holy Spirit who fights *for* us. The key is learning to abide in Christ. In John 15, Jesus describes the Christian life in terms of His being the vine and our being the branches, emphasizing our need to be so rooted in Him that we draw power, understanding, strength, and wisdom as a natural outgrowth of this union. A stronger love for and desire to be attached to Christ is absolute.

Unfortunately, many of us are not prepared for our Carnal Corral confrontations. When we became Christians, we were told to follow a formula and everything would fall into place. Step out of line, and a quote from the Bible would fix everything. With that promise under our belts, we went out to face any foe or obstacle. Romans 8:31 says that if God is for us, who can stand against us? We are more than conquerors. We even felt cocky—almost invincible.

So many of us buy into the Christian life like a lawman strapping on a six-shooter and pinning on a badge. We're gonna clean up the town because we have all the authority in the world. We act as if God has hired us to be on His side and deputized us to carry out His law and order.

And that's the entire issue. We act as if *we* need to keep the law. That attitude only brings condemnation and strain in our spirits. We are no longer under the law, so we needn't keep it And God doesn't need us to keep it for Him. The enemy knows this and he will resort to anything to draw us into a fight on his terms.

The result of fighting battles your way is defeat. That's why there are so many walking wounded Christians. They've gone into battle inappropriately armed and have found themselves, quite naturally, in their own gunfight at the Carnal Corral. No one ever explained to them that God is not looking for lawmen but "gracemen." Badges mean nothing. Jesus means everything.

Grace has come to prevent me from going one-on-one with the enemy. Jesus now handles my confrontations at the Carnal Corral. That's the difference.

So when you plan to go out and fight the evil in the world, leave the badge and gun home. The Carnal Corral has been the road to Boot Hill for many a believer. Instead, learn the secret of "'Not by might nor by power, but by My Spirit,' says the Lord Almighty" (Zech. 4:6). Allow Christ to so control your being that He will fight your fights and face your foes. You needn't go to the Carnal Corral at all, ever again, when you're firmly rooted in the vine. So save yourself a walk. You wouldn't be much help anyway.

4

Trench Warfare

World War I was famous for its unique style of fighting: trench warfare. Ground was won and lost inch by inch as armies battled each other from trench to trench. There were no long-range missiles or air support, just the old-fashioned way of fighting. Armies literally dug in and stayed that way for years. When someone decided to advance, it was mostly hand-to-hand combat. It was a tedious way of slugging it out.

This outdated World War I method of warfare is similar to how the church confronts "the enemy" today. We burrow ourselves in our churches, trying to protect our territory, shooting from our trench, and hardly ever advancing on the enemy. Trench warfare mentality tries to preserve territory already won. It's a much safer, defensive position.

Yet, the psychology of war is a funny thing. We keep fighting people we've never met, usually on someone else's orders. Our perception is that the enemies are so radically different from us, they're worth eliminating. Or at least worth not liking very much. Not unlike how the church perceives its enemies.

Unfortunately, much of current church mentality likes to define those who are different as "the enemy," and responds to the world (and other churches) as if it were engaged in trench warfare. The current crusade lists as infidels all humanists, secular humanists, atheists, agnostics, democrats, feminists, liberals, and certain Christian denominations. The list goes on ad infinitum. The righteous are in the pew; the unrighteous are in the world. Location is everything. Sounds more like a real estate seminar than church policy.

And guess what? There's another church not too far away that's also in a trench. They may be our ally, but we're not sure because we can't get out of our trench long enough to go over there and find out. How many times do lo-cal churches come together, putting aside de-nominational and doctrinal differences, and attempt to advance together on the real enemy? If the world is to know that we are Christians by our love for one another (John 13:35), how does staying entrenched within our individual territories reflect this? At times, it appears that the church competes more with itself than with the world.

Somehow, we feel that if we were to leave our trenches, the "enemy" might plan a sneak attack at that very moment and take the ground that we've held for who knows how long. And all that work of just sitting here in this trench will have been for nothing. Can't risk that, can we? Instead, we remain in the trench, fighting a war which the enemy may have left years ago. This reminds me of stories about men who were found hiding in remote jungle locations in the South Pacific several years after World War II, unaware that the war had ended. They had continued the fight against an enemy that no longer existed be-cause they were so far removed from any com-munication.

As Christians, the more we compete

against each other, the less we compete against
Satan for the lives of others. And that's pre-
cisely what has happened in our church world
today. We'd rather dig deeper foxholes and
trenches than climb out into the battle to encounter the people Jesus wants us to meet face
to face. Just because they don't think or look or
act like us, and they may not even like us, still,
they are not the enemy. We have only one real
enemy. And he is not going to come to our door-
way to let us know where to find him, especially when we are out to defeat him. We know
the enemy is out there. Where else would he
go? We pop our heads out and get fired upon, so
he must be out there, right?

Wouldn't it be interesting to find out that
those shots might not have been coming from
the enemy at all! Rather, it could be that your
ally has been taking shots at you all this time
to keep you in your trench, maybe to mislead
you so he could advance on your territory. The
recent televangelist scandals brought out the
worst in the church, not just by those who were
caught in impropriety, but by those who decided to shoot at the others from the safety of
their trenches. Their behavior and attitudes
were indicative of how out of touch much of

American evangelical Christianity is with the world.

Some in church trench warfare mistake members of their own units as the enemy! Someone who doesn't like a form of Christian music or another's cultural expression of worship feels it necessary to shoot down this group, which is only trying to fight the real enemy in their own way. It gets pretty confusing when generals give orders to fire on their own men. A number of casualties are often due to friendly fire.

One of the reasons that our culture has been described as post-Christian is because believers have opted to remain in a safe environment and engage each other and the world in this trench warfare. Ideally, we allies should come to the bargaining table to resolve our differences. Tradition, pride, fear, denomination, and a host of other things keep us separated. We need to find common ground so that we can fight the enemy together. The things that keep us separated are not as significant as the thing that will unite us, namely Jesus, particularly in light of the advancing enemy. He is the only one who can fight the enemy on this battle-ground and be victorious. Sheep can never protect each other. Only the Shepherd can protect the flock. But we've been so busy trying to keep our flocks and ourselves protected from the world (and each other) that the world no longer knows we're around. And if they don't know we're around, then surely they aren't hearing or experiencing the message of Jesus' love.

Jesus wants us all to get out of the trench and take back the land currently in the hands of the enemy.

So, Christian, get out of the trench. We don't need bigger foxholes to protect us from danger. Jesus said He would do that. He promises His peace and His presence in the midst of danger (John 16:33). The apostle John underscores this by stating, "He who is in you is greater than he who is in the world" (1 John 4:4). Instead of sitting in a trench, we should be standing in the pulpits of our vocations, schools, or on the streets, representing Jesus to the world.

If we do this, our encounter with the world will often lead to resolution and reconciliation, not retreat and entrenchment. Some battles need not be fought. Jesus wants us to offer peace, not tribulation and strife. The peace He offers is not the kind offered by the world (John

14:27). Paul emphasizes in 2 Corinthians 5:18–20 that God was, in Christ, reconciling the world to Himself. Our task should be similar—to reestablish friendship between God and man. That's the role of the reconciler. It's an impossible task with a trench warfare mindset.

So if you've been in the foxhole too long, begin negotiations by waving a white flag and talking with the "enemy." Who knows, the guy may not be as bad as you thought. He might end up becoming your friend. Or your brother. And you may finally realize who the real enemy is.

5

Beasts of Burden

Most of us have the pack-rat tendency to save things rather than throw them away. Some of us like to store things in the attic until there's no more room, or stuff a closet until it resembles the local landfill.

We have a love affair with junk. We just can't seem to throw anything away. There's always some reason to keep it, like sentiment or perceived value. Or guilt, particularly if someone asks us to keep their junk for them. So we store it in our house, thereby adding to our already overcrowded attics and basements.

Unfortunately, this accumulation of junk doesn't stop with cluttering our houses. We often clutter our spiritual lives, too, with junk for which we no longer have any use or that others ask us to carry. In doing this, we carry a lot of extra weight, both emotionally *and* spiritually, and shoulder responsibilities that aren't ours in the first place. It's amazing how we often complicate our lives with unnecessary baggage while traveling along our spiritual journeys. Like a bunch of wandering spiritual nomads, we are constantly searching for a place to rest our emotionally drained bodies laboring under the load of unnecessary baggage and others' expectations.

How did we get loaded down with all these things in the first place?

Think back to your first months, weeks, even days as a new believer. There was so much to assimilate. You couldn't wait to attend the latest meeting, teaching, or concert. You were like a sponge, soaking up everything that resembled anything Christian. You wanted to learn everything overnight and hurry past the stage of maturity that requires waiting rather than doing. You didn't understand that in God's economy, time is as important as speed.

You didn't know about using proper discernment to differentiate between the good stuff and the junk. It didn't matter. It came right from another believer's mouth, so it must have been right. Or so you thought.

In effect, this particular mindset in some Christian circles has transformed many believers into modern day beasts of burden—encouraged, trained, and used to carry the extra baggage of conformity to someone else's rules and lifestyle.

Conformity is so deceiving. It forces me to take my eyes off Jesus to focus on others. The Christian life then becomes an illusion because I can't be what others are; I wasn't meant for that. What's funny is that *they* aren't even what they appear to be!

Indeed, conformity is a heavy burden because I now carry not just my burden, but yours too.

Worst of all, we especially like to assign new believers to this beast-of-burden mentality by strapping our favorite "ism" to their back. Maybe it's our favorite burden to carry, so we automatically assume that every believer should carry this load as well.

What a privilege. It's so nice for us to think of others, isn't it? We enjoy having them carry the same load we like to carry. As such, some new (and old) believers feel like they're not part of God's kingdom, but the animal kingdom—performing in a circus or zoo, contained by bars or cages, and gawked at by the crowd.

Usually, when we carry things around unnecessarily, our backs ache from the exertion and our spirits become weighted down with the cares and anxieties that come with this burden. We feel terrible. And we look a wreck.

Our Christian experience ultimately becomes defined by how much we can carry from place to place. We load upon ourselves the cares and worries, the latest theologies, and concerns or fights against the enemy. Just like pack horses.

Unfortunately, the weight of all this stuff restricts the freedom Christ offers, and our identities suffer as a result. Freedom unshackles the one enslaved, so that we start with new identities (2 Cor. 5:17) and new minds (Rom. 12:2). The slate is clean, and so should be the closets of our spiritual lives.

Jesus understood that putting a burden on someone is a form of control and power. He confronted the Pharisees for their hypocrisy about His healings on the Sabbath, the woman caught in adultery, and other incidents. He constantly saw people weighted down with loads imposed on them by religious people.

Ideally, we should be defined by how *unen-cumbered* we are, not by how much we can load upon ourselves. The Christian life is not a weight lifting contest.

Are you carrying an unnecessary burden? What can you do?

Understand that Jesus wants to carry the load for you. And that we are complete in Him. He admonished us in Matthew 11:28–29 to carry His yoke, for His burden is light. He understood that we have a tendency to carry unnecessary cares and anxieties, whether self-imposed or imposed by others. He alone can provide the necessary strength to offset the things that would wear us down (1 Peter 5:7).

Jesus promised us freedom, not just from sin and its penalty, but from other believers and their rules, the very things that inhibit attaining the abundant life. Freedom sets not only our backs straight, but our vision as well.

We needn't saddle ourselves or other believers with burdens we like to carry. The only burden we should bear is each other's, thereby fulfilling the law of Christ.

6

Security in an Insecure World

The newspaper was filled with much of the same stories today—another savings and loan office was closed down; someone was laid off from his job after twenty years; another indictment against one of our "prominent" government leaders. Once stable elements in our society are beginning to crumble.

If that's not bad enough, our trusted, all-American symbols of Mom, apple pie, and the flag have also fallen on tough times. According to a recent national study, Mom now ranks twenty-eighth as being the most influential person in her child's life; apple pie may contain alar; and the flag is burned or used as a door-mat.

"In God We Trust" is still inscribed on our coins. When will our currency no longer be allowed in public schools under the separation of church and state?

The cracks in the dike are getting bigger, and we've run out of fingers to plug them. My, things *have* changed!

Our former rock-like symbols of security now seem like pebbles on the landscape of our culture. We stumble over them rather than stand on them. To many, security apart from a dead bolt or a million in the bank, is virtually nonexistent.

Still, everyone is looking for it, but it remains elusive to most. Security has become harder and harder to find because we really don't understand where to look for it.

As our world nosedives out of control due to drug terrorism, rampant crime, and families in turmoil, insecurity increases. Fear becomes the by-product of a life or society out of control. And people will look anywhere, do anything to attain security.

Our insecurity is not caused by the presence of fear; it's caused by the absence of control. Paradoxically, the Bible suggests that security is best realized when we relinquish *our* pursuit of being in control and put our trust in God. Jesus best describes the issue of control in Matthew 6, detailing God's concern and care for the smallest of animals and flowers to underscore the importance of human lives in God's sight. Understanding that perspective, Jesus says, should give us confidence and rest. When the world is unraveling before us, Jesus asks to look at life with another set of eyes. That's the ultimate security.

On the other hand, many Christians have a different perspective of the security issue altogether. They like to debate it in terms of the salvation experience. Quite frankly, security (eternal or otherwise) is best understood when viewed as a simple trust relationship and not as a theological point. Understanding the theology only brings us to the point of belief. Trusting in the theology makes it a fact. Trusting in God makes it a reality. It's not a question of whether one can lose one's salvation, but of whether God can lose control.

Frankly, I'll take my chances with God in control. Debating an issue like security is like debating an understanding of a symptom rather than the reality of a cure. God doesn't need to win a debate, only humans do.

I am eternally secure, not because I believe I am, but because of who God is and what He has promised. This takes the burden to understand a theological debate off me and puts the emphasis on my relationship with God and the fact that He's in control. It's a lot neater that way.

Some people feel they are eternally secure; others feel they can lose their salvation. Security is not something you can hold on to, lose, or work to attain. Instead, it gives me confidence to be in God's presence without working for His approval, without worrying or wondering if He's going to throw me out. It's supposed to be a big relief; we've questioned it so much that it's turned into a big fear.

Fear is one of the greatest means of control. It enables unscrupulous people (sometimes church members) to build power bases (even congregations) to do their bidding. Some of our fear is also self-inflicted. We're afraid to believe that God wants freedom for us because that would mean responsibility, love, and sharing, and we fear those things. Sadly, in doing so, we fear the very things that can remove the fear. Ultimately, we fear God instead of loving Him, unaware that love builds security while fear breeds insecurity.

Fear erects fences in a land of no boundaries, imaginary lines over which we dare not cross. As we approach the line, we hold our breath to see how God will react.

Which brings us back to the issue of security.

Because our world encourages us to hold on to our lives and hoard our possessions, we need a special understanding of security. God's perspective on security is for us to stand guard over nothing, to have a house with no valuables, a vault with no money. If there's nothing to take, then there's nothing to watch.

I learned long ago that what is out of my control falls into the realm of Romans 8:30–31. We need to grasp the significance of that passage so that when we find ourselves holding on to things too tightly, we can have the freedom to let go. Funny how the world would want to hold on to the things that can't be controlled and reject the things that need no control.

Imagine a fist made so tightly that the knuckles turn white. That's how hard we try to hold on to the things we value too much. The tendency is to hold on tighter, reminiscent of the way monkeys are trapped. The monkey easily fits its empty hand into a hollowed out gourd for food. But when he makes a fist to pull out the food, the monkey can't get the food, or its fist, out!

You'd think the monkey would just let go of the food and slip out his hand. Not so. Instead, he continues to hold on to the food, preventing his own escape. Ultimately, he traps himself.

Before we think the monkey stupid, we should look at the way we attempt to hold on to the things that will eventually ensnare us. If the bait is enticing, we sometimes refuse to let go, even when we know there's danger.

God's way out of the trap is for us to relinquish control. Only then can we free our hands for what God holds out to us. In this way, the thing we let go of no longer fulfills our desires. Only after we've let go can God use us. He will not hold on to us if we prefer to hold on to something else.

So I have learned that whatever I cannot control, I let loose or release. This frees me to carry on God's work in God's will, so that He is in control. That's all God ever wants. And when that happens, we sense a security in our spirit that we often struggle unsuccessfully to achieve in our flesh.

Security. A strange word and hard to find.

Yet we can only find it when we stop striving and start releasing. That's trust. It's certainly not the world's pattern.

Fortunately, God's patterns are cut from a different cloth.

7

Parable of the Cattle Drive

Remember those old movies about the cattle drives from Texas to Kansas? I used to love to watch them. There was always plenty of action and adventure. And you could always count on a stampede. Something would spook those cows—the bad guys trying to rustle a few, bad weather, an ill-timed gunshot, or just some howling coyotes. It didn't take much. Inevitably, someone would get caught in the middle of the stampede and lose his life, wagons would be bowled over, or some of the cows would be killed. It could get pretty messy.

Funny how one minute all the cows would be down for the evening, resting peacefully, and then, all of a sudden, from nowhere, the stampede would begin. It took only a few cows to get all the others going. Then, everyone would follow—thousands of cows running wildly in all directions. Imagine, just a couple of cows to start all that damage.

Can you picture one cow turning to another cow and asking, "Where are we goin' in such a rush?" "I don't know," replies the second cow. "I'm just followin' the guy up there. Must be important. Otherwise, why would we be running so fast?"

I don't have to watch many of those westerns anymore because life in the church can easily resemble a western! We have professional stampeders, right in our midst, who will bolt from just about anything and get others to follow them blindly. They create a fuss that affects everyone around them. Let's identify some of these stampeders.

One is the sacred cow. Now, the sacred cow is a strange animal. He's been around forever and has had the respect of the herd for a number of reasons. He has always known just the right trail to follow to find food for the other cows, so many of the cows trust him. That's reassuring. The sacred cow also stands as a symbol of all the herd has been through in the past to reach its present destination. In this sense, the cow becomes more than just another animal; he becomes untouchable, even if there's starvation in the camp. People would rather die than kill the sacred cow.

Because of his track record, a lot of other cows revere the grass where he grazes. So any cow who suggests grazing somewhere else usually gets ignored or even condemned. "We've always grazed here," they say. "This is the best grass anywhere. How could it get any better?"

Regrettably, the sacred cow knows only one way. Although he's often been right, lately, he hasn't followed the weather patterns to know if there's been any change at the watering hole or grazing area with which he's so familiar. He just keeps going back, not considering that the well may dry up or that the grass is insufficient to support the herd. Neither he nor the rest of the cows will discover this until it has actually happened. And then sometimes it's too late. The consequences can be tragic.

In a sense, the sacred cow stampedes the herd into believing him. It's a different kind of stampede, which makes it all the more dangerous since it's not readily apparent. It's still deadly.

Not keeping up with the times leads to a sad ending for the sacred cow. What's sadder is that his lack of foresight can result in a similar fate for the other cows: They die or become of no use to anyone. The road used by the sacred cow is often marked by the carcasses of other cows.

Another stampeder is the bullheaded cow. He acts more like a bull than a cow. He swaggers like a bull and throws his weight around like a bull, but he's only a cow. He doesn't want to admit that, because he likes to be different and bullheaded and loves to annoy the other cows. He doesn't like to follow anyone and, as a result, always wanders off simply because he'd rather blaze a trail of his own. He thinks he knows better than the cowboy, who, regardless of how many times the bullheaded cow strays, always brings him back to the herd.

Regrettably, this cow often leads other cows along on his meanderings. More often than not, the bullheaded cow and his pals get lost, disrupting the schedule of the drive. On their selfish pursuits, one day, this cow will get himself and his friends into trouble. He'll sepa-rate himself from the rest of the herd and run into a pack of hungry wolves who will attack when he's weakest and alone. No cowboy will be around to save him then. But that's what he gets for being so bullheaded.

At other times, the bullheaded cow thinks he knows more than the cowboy about a cattle drive and decides to challenge the cowboy's au-thority with a stampede of his own. Because he's got such a convincing, forceful personality, other cows follow him. Many times the stam-pede is so large, it splits the herd. Some cows can't keep up with the confusion and eventu-ally get lost and die. They need the stability of the herd and the guidance of the cowboy. The bullheaded cow just likes to run off on his own and knows nothing about nurturing the other cows.

Ironically, both the sacred cow and the bullheaded cow are part of the same drive and herd. Each thinks the other is out of place with his desire for the herd. The sacred cow lives in the past and, as a result, forfeits the future. The bullheaded cow could care less about the past or the future and lives for the present. They're different, yet so similar.

You might want to look at the herd you're in. Don't let the sacred cow stampede you into a certain direction because it's the only familiar way to the watering hole and it's always been there. Things may have changed, and you may need to change your course to reach your destination. It never hurts to reevaluate your methods in bringing the herd through.

And don't follow the bullheaded cow who wants to stray from the herd. He's not interested in getting to the watering hole; he's interested in doing his own thing. Remember, there may be wolves out there, just waiting for the right time to pounce on an unsuspecting cow. Anyone for a roast beef dinner?

Ideally, if you're a cow on a drive, your best bet is to follow the cowboy. He'll know if the watering hole is still there. If not, he'll find another. And he'll be able to bring back the cows that want to leave the herd for their own adventure. Stay with the cowboy. Along the way, you may need to make some route adjustments, do some strange things for the good of the herd, things you've never done. That's all right. The idea is to get to the destination without losing any cows.

Ultimately, the herd does a lot better when

following the cowboy and not listening to the beef of either the sacred or bullheaded cow. There's so much more space to roam and feed on the route mapped out by the cowboy, the one responsible for the herd's safety.

8

Ministry Is a Funny Word

Ministry is a funny word. It's commonly used to define something that I have. But, it's not that at all. Ministry is not something I do, but something which happens in the heart of someone else. The evidence of God working in lives as a result of my efforts is the real indication of a ministry.

People are always looking for a quality of life that is elusive. A true ministry will lead others to that quality of life, not necessarily build a quality of life for you. The tangible result is changed lives.

Coming to an understanding of that definition of ministry was very freeing to me. It took away the burden of needing "results" and shifted the emphasis to the work of the Holy Spirit in a person's life. My "ministry" only becomes ministry when something happens to someone else's heart as a result of God working in it.

The great news is this: I really don't *have* a ministry; I *am* one.

No, I'm not nit-picking words. A lot of people may feel they have a ministry, but have never really been called. They just went. It's like the old adage about a leader: He who thinks he's a leader and looks behind to find no one following is only going for a walk.

So what do I look for in a ministry? And how do I know I'm not just going for a walk?

First, you can always tell if someone has the wrong concept of ministry when the leader seems more blessed than the recipients. For example, I recently heard a preacher use that oft-quoted Scripture in Luke 6:38 to ask for support of his ministry. "Give, and it will be given to you: good measure, pressed down, shaken together, and running over will be put into your bosom." The person quoting the

Scripture inferred that if you gave to his ministry, God would reward your faithfulness and repay you a hundredfold. And wouldn't God honor His Word?

I never doubt that God honors His Word. I often doubt that He will honor it the way some say He will.

Somehow, I felt that the framing of that proposition was a bit convoluted—asking me for money so that I'll get blessed when, in fact, the real reason he asked for my money was so that he would get blessed, wasn't it? That seems a bit more honest.

I think many people feel this way with many fund-raising approaches. To those carefully scrutinizing believers in particular, these tactics seem very suspicious, however honest and well intentioned.

Sadly, solid biblical principles of giving are often twisted to solicit funds rather than to explain the heart of God toward resource channeling, and are tied to a quid pro quo, namely that your giving will precipitate a gain on your balance sheet.

Second, you know that not much is happening when it's obvious that you spend more time and energy than are justified trying to sustain the memory of your ministry based on past achievements. The memories of ministry-past can carry a lot of weight, and, if carefully presented, can give the impression that something dead is still alive and worthy of your support. Collecting funds for ministries has become an art, at best.

Third, other people will recognize and validate your ministry; you won't have to say anything. Changed lives, not a change in your agency, will determine your success.

My saying I have a ministry doesn't necessarily mean I have one. When I hear some people talk about their ministry, it's almost as if they purchased one in a catalog. Or they're starting a business: Go to an attorney, file the papers, and you're incorporated. Anyone can have a ministry. Right?

Hanging out a shingle is the way to start a business; hanging out your heart is the way to start a ministry.

People will be attracted to the ministry that offers an approach to life that can sustain them. They'll look for something very important in you: the ability just to be real. The world is looking for real people with unreal love in a real world. Ministry will happen when the human heart is touched by this unreal love.

I learned long ago that ministry happens best when I approach each situation with this attitude: How can I be a servant and am I acting out of love? My role and responsibility in ministry is not to get a hundredfold of anything, pressed down and shaken together, but rather to be used to cause a stirring in the human heart.

So the next time you say, "This is my ministry," think about it. Do you really have one? And what heart has been touched or changed? *Ministry is not what I do, but what's been done to me*. That's God's perspective. What's yours?

9

Controlling Interest

Positioning is a hot word in today's business vocabulary. Simply put, if we want to control or impact a certain market, then we need to communicate an image of ourselves or our product that will make an unforgettable impression on our target audience and motivate them to action.

Corporations and individuals spend millions each year to position themselves. The right strategy and campaign will increase profits, as well as other tangible benefits, everything from increased sales to increased productivity to expansion into other markets to more personal power. Positioning is the key to establishing the identity of an individual or business, which is the key to success. If your plan fails, you may not get a second try. The person or business that fails to position itself correctly is in big trouble.

It seems, though, that positioning is not reserved exclusively for the business world. Have you ever stopped to think how much like corporations we are? Individually, we too jockey for position and power. It's bad enough when it's in the world; it's sad when it involves the church.

Yes, we position ourselves for power in the church—power over others, and sometimes, power over God. Of course, we would never admit to this power trip, particularly over God. But often, that's how we act.

You might ask, "How are people trying to exercise power over me?" Like positioning campaigns, it happens very subtly. You may not even notice it. That's why it's called positioning and not pushing.

People position themselves to gain control, whether of a market, a product line, or other people, which is when the real problem arises.

This desire to take control of others usually results in acquiescence or confrontation. The battle is between those who would control and dominate and those who prefer the freedom to live their lives as they understand them.

When Christians struggle for power, they usually cloak their actions in spiritual terms to take the edge off their involvement. "Being wise as a serpent" is used to cover up a business deal in which you lied and cheated to gain control of a company. Many things have been done in Christ's name to exercise control over people. Maybe you have been involved personally in one or two cases.

History is full of examples. The New Testament had its share of confrontations among spiritual leaders. Paul and Barnabas split in a dispute over whether to take John Mark along on a missionary journey. They began as a team, but this decision ended the teamwork. Who was right? Or wrong? Scripture doesn't say, which might be good indication that *both were right*. Perhaps Paul and Barnabas needed to go separate ways in order for God to use them in different places and for different reasons. Perhaps *John Mark wasn't the issue at all but*

*was, instead, the instrument God used to sepa-
rate them.* It could be that John Mark was
where he was supposed to be all along, and so
were Paul and Barnabas.

Interestingly, though, neither man tried to
position himself to be right or above the other
in the pecking order. They just disagreed and
let it go at that. No one wanted to be in charge.
But neither did they want to back away from
what they felt God calling them to do.

Each did the right thing: He followed God
for himself. They did not seek to control each
other or pull rank. Their desire was to expand
the kingdom, not prevent each other from running the race.

Often, we find ourselves in similar confrontations with other believers, and the part-
ing shots are "You're wrong if you don't follow
God the way I follow Him." People disagree and
often separate on points of theology, musical
preferences, personal grooming. We think we're
right and feel we're right for you too. Not only
do we lead people to water, but we try to drink
it for them.

Many in the church are not satisfied to interpret differences as a signal that God is mov-

ing through people differently; they want to interpret these differences as God taking sides. And, naturally, He's on their side.

It's never a question of who's right or wrong. Instead, it's a question of each person needing to listen to God. Both Paul and Barnabas went ahead and served Christ, not their own purpose.

This lordship trip assumes that God is on my side in every debate and matter of difference and is used as a way for believers to feel superior to fellow believers. The motive and spirit behind this action is judgment and victory, not understanding and reconciliation. For some reason, those who exercise this attitude feel that to give in is to lose control. And control is the name of the game.

Unfortunately, we also try to assume this lordship over unbelievers who really don't understand what we mean when a Christian "suggests" how they ought to live their lives. Some believers feel superior to those outside the faith, attempting to claim some authority over them by invoking the name of Christ and proceeding to tell them how they should live. These unbelievers get caught in the crossfire.

At other times, they're casualities of war between believers.

So stop trying to get the controlling interest on anyone or positioning for a good spot in the kingdom. Jesus' answer will probably be the same for you as it was for John and James when their mother positioned for them. There's no room for king of the mountain in kingdom building. We already have one. Forget about positioning and start petitioning.

10

Solitary Confinement

Have you ever spent time in jail? No? Well, neither have I. At least not the kind that has four walls and bars! Unfortunately, though, much of our present church culture and lifestyle imprisons people. But it's a different sort of prison. No bars or doors or guards or barbed wire.

We've put ourselves into solitary confinement—that realm of the spirit that makes no room for Christ's life to take root but, instead, requires our faith be an imitation of another's.

The Christian should be free from this,
but frequently he's not. That's why we have so
many lonely and distraught believers. I hear
them every day as they call in to the many talk
shows available on Christian radio. You ought
to hear some of these calls. It's tragic because
it's so unnecessary. A person's faith should free
him or her to experience new life in Christ, not
keep him or her in bondage.

For too long, believers have been impris-
oned under the oppressive weight of their own
lifestyles or misconceptions of living the Christian life. They need to know that they can do
more than just walk around in the prison court-
yard for a few hours each day; they can walk
right out of the prison!

We need a massive prison riot in the
church. But first, let's identify some of the cells
in our solitary confinement compound.

One cell is located on the bottom floor of
the faith. It's called "this is my church." The
"this is my church" person feels so attached to
his particular church that he has to defend it
against any intrusion by another believer different from himself in worship or in desire for outreach. This person has been there since the

church began and cannot bear to relinquish control to those who would do things different from how they've been done before.

This person wouldn't recognize a move of God, even with a "For Sale" sign in front. He's incapable of understanding that God can and will work differently at times to achieve His purposes. God does not ask for our endorsement of His plan, just our obedience to it. So, because the "this is my church" person can't see this move of God, he assumes that the activities he finds so uncomfortable are not really a move of God at all, but merely something at odds with his personal faith.

If a church is led by a person in this cell, eventually no one will move, and they will all stagnate. God can't steer a parked car. He can't use them as His "vehicle" if they're unwilling to go where He tells them. Once they're on the road, they certainly can't find something they're not looking for. And the "this is my church" person will never stop to ask for directions or even consult a road map. The result is being lost, though they think they're headed in the right direction. That can get pretty lonely. Eventually, they imprison themselves in a lifestyle lacking in any meaningful contacts.

Another cell block is the "instant replay." Here, believers are always going back to the videotape to see how it was done in the past or to analyze how their plays could have been better. The problem is that they never get past the replays. Their ideas worked great back then, just look at the film footage. What a run! What a pass! How can you compare those great moments in the past with the present or the future? The "instant replay" people are frozen in time, much like the pictures to which they constantly refer.

Because they lack vision, the people in this cell forfeit the future. Looking back is too much fun, and it's so much easier. They can't enjoy looking at anything else. It's just not the same. Here, too, people get tired of seeing the same old thing and begin to leave. One day, they suddenly notice that no one is left behind. So they are all alone with their memories and their past. And that's all. The future can be pretty empty and lonely with no one around.

Then there's the "pacesetter's cell." These are people who think they're moving ahead with God because they're always changing, supposedly to relate to the world around them or to the latest "in" theology. Changing with

the times. Changing with the culture. Changing with the Spirit. But if the change is merely
on the outside, not the inside, then rearranging
the furniture of our spiritual lives will not do.
Change doesn't change people; only Jesus does.
The pacesetter can wind up so ahead of everyone else that he is all alone. Or so busy changing to relate that he relates to no one. Both
instances keep him apart from people and
result in another locked-out relationship.

That's why Jesus calls us to change from
within, not just alter our circumstances. If our
actions change because the Spirit has renewed
and changed our minds, that's great. But if it's
only our actions that change and not our
hearts, then we're simply living out religion.
And we have too much religion in America.

The world offers its own brand of solitary
confinement without the church having to add
its own. Believers need to learn that the only
One who can unlock their door is Jesus Himself. Others would keep us locked up in their
points of theology, their denominational idio-
syncrasies, or their church politics. Jesus offers
us a full pardon from the solitary confinement
of our spirit, wipes clean the slate against us,
and then, as in the witness relocation program,

gives us a completely new identity so that we are dead to our former lives. Our past will never affect us.

So if you're locked up in solitary confinement today, you can break loose from the things that keep you there. A relationship with Jesus will free your spirit and your mind so as not to conform to prisoners of the church or the world. You've had the key to escape all along and never knew it.

It's never too late to use it; it fits every lock.

**PART
TWO**

A Unique
Identity

"And to put on the new self, created to be like God" (Eph. 4:24).

Parable of
the Fertilizer

We're all familiar with the salt and light analogies Christ uses in Matthew 5:13–16 to describe His followers. "You are the salt of the earth; but if the salt loses its flavor, how shall it be seasoned? It is then good for nothing but to be thrown out and trampled underfoot by men. You are the light of the world. A city that is set on a hill cannot be hidden. Nor do they light a lamp and put it under a basket, but on a lampstand, and it gives light to all who are in the house. Let your light so shine before men, that they may see your good works and glorify your Father in heaven."

In that portion of the Sermon on the Mount, Jesus describes in earthly terms the distinguishing characteristics of those who would be His disciples: They would flavor and act as a preservative to society and dispel darkness so as to illumine godliness. The result of all this salting and lighting is that our behavior should point people to God, not to us.

But in our present society, we are more like fertilizer than salt and light. Let's consider the similarity!

Fertilizer is to be spread evenly over the land to enrich and nourish the soil and encourage growth of all that is planted there. Fertilizer is useful, even necessary, to replenish the land with those nutrients that make it productive. Without fertilizer, the land may not sustain the growth of good plants. But weeds don't have that problem; they don't need fertilizer. They grow everywhere and eventually choke the growth of good plants. Fertilizer helps control the weeds by creating the right climate for good plants to grow so that weeds don't take over the land.

On the other hand, if fertilizer is stockpiled for too long, without being spread throughout the land and used as the enriching agent it's meant to be, it begins to fester, smell, even attract flies. Instead of contributing to the growth of the land, it becomes useless. Things are great in the one area where all the fertilizer is, but outside that area, everything else is dying. And the weeds begin to take over.

Christians are very much like fertilizer. They were meant to be spread throughout the land as an enriching agent, not to remain in one area. They are to provide valuable nutrients that bring life to barren lives, and aid in the growth of those who can't make it alone. A Christian is more than salt and light to the world because society needs more than just preserving—it needs replenishing. That's the job of fertilizer. That's our unique calling. Ideally, we should be known by the way in which we enrich our world by our presence.

On the other hand, if Christians stockpile in one area without being the enriching agents they were meant to be, they begin to fester, even smell, if you know what I mean. It's not a pleasant sight or aroma when that happens. And if you happen to be downwind of them. . . .

First of all, ask yourself if you're acting like

salt. Are you preserving the land? Or do you remain in the shaker and clump together with the rest of the salt? You know what happens then. It sure is hard to shake loose, isn't it? And is your light pleasant to be around, or is it blinding? Just what do you illuminate anyway?

Lastly, are you acting like fertilizer? Are you spreading yourself out to enrich the land or stockpiling yourself with other Christians?

By the way, what's that I smell? Just thought I'd ask.

2

The Me-Attitudes

Author and social critic Tom Wolfe coined the phrase "the Me Decade" to describe the American cultural/social environment of the 1970s. It became the decade of introspection and self-gratification, a pendulum swing from the '60s when everyone was into rights for everyone else and disillusioned with traditional values. This disillusionment left gaping holes in peoples' hearts that needed to be filled with meaning and identity.

After such an intense attempt in the '60s to create a more perfect society, the mood changed in the '70s and people just wanted to get on with their own thing. As a result, a grow-

ing awareness of spiritual purpose left over
from the '60s, though not understood in biblical terms, was wed with the desire for self-
gratification in the '70s to create a fertile
seedbed for new American religious experi-
ences. Obviously, altruism was no longer high
on anyone's list.

The new motto of the American dream became "looking out for number one." Building
for the future suddenly meant building for *my*
future, not for the corporate good. Society was
redefined to mean "me," instead of "me along
with everyone else." Commitment became
equated with bondage.

To make life easier, we became a disposable society. Everything from diapers to the unborn could be thrown away. How ironic that
one industry grew in response to wanted children and another in response to unwanted children. This "disposable" mentality has become
imbedded in the mindset of the American cultural experience. Whenever something loses its
purpose, we get rid of it.

The '70s also saw the end of Vietnam, the
Beatles, and Elvis. And some say God. Lately,
though, some people still believe that God is
dead and Elvis is still alive! This alone is a good

indicator of the general consensus of how God and the Bible relate to many Americans. My, things have changed.

Unfortunately, the cultural revolution of the 1970s with its emphasis on self-indulgence also invaded the church, and the effects have lasted through the '80s and into the '90s. More and more, the church began to take on the personality of the American culture, becoming more interested in self-realization and individuality at the expense of the corporate good than in the biblical model of service to others and interdependence within the body.

This self-realization thinking flies in the face of what Jesus taught in the Beatitudes, that God's people aren't necessarily the strongest, bravest, biggest, or most independent, only the most in love with God and the most desirous of doing His will. In one account, Jesus says that we should rejoice when we encounter persecution for His name's sake, since we will have our reward in heaven. In the instant gratification attitude of our culture, that's not soon enough for most people. We want our reward now. Selfishness always wants everything now.

A society of self-indulgent people does not like the idea of self-denial, death, and the cross.

So it has decided to reshape some of the biblical concepts of servanthood and freedom to fit the newly formed concept of the American dream of service for self and freedom from responsibility.

We have secularized the Beatitudes and renamed them the Me-Attitudes to fit more appropriately our new form of secularized religion. Here are some of them:

Blessed are the macho,
for they will take (not inherit) the land.

Blessed are those who hunger and
thirst for power,
for they will get to the top and climb over
anyone to achieve that goal.

Blessed are those who show no mercy,
for they expect no mercy in return.

Blessed are the deceitful in heart,
for they are their own god.

Blessed are the warmongers,
for they will be called the sons of strife.

Blessed are those who persecute others
for their righteousness,
for theirs is their own hell—to live
with themselves.

The Me-Attitudes have become the driving religious experience for many in our world today. Concentrating on oneself always drives us to look inward. But, usually, what we see is not worth talking about because when we honestly examine our hearts, we see what Jeremiah knew: that the heart of man is wicked.

Self-directedness is a terrible form of slavery from which Jesus came to release us (John 5:43–44; 7:18). So look at your life. Are you a Beatitude or a Me-Attitude person? Maybe it's time to look at Jesus once again, not our culture or a religious experience, to give us a perspective of life that will bring true freedom and self-realization.

A Vagrant Faith

"This is not my home. I'm just passin' through."

How many times have you heard a Christian use that statement in relation to his ultimate destiny? We casually (and sometimes snobbishly) use it to communicate our reluctance to identify with "worldly practices" in order to stand in contrast to what is going on around us. It's supposed to put things into perspective. But perspective is far from practice. We're great at saying things but deficient in actually doing them.

We're so busy conforming more to our culture than to Jesus, or trying to make Jesus fit our culture, that we've lost the purpose of our faith.

One important perspective we've lost is that of the vagrant faith: to be given everything, yet own nothing. The vagrant faith understands that poverty and ownership are part and parcel the same lifestyle. In Christ I have all, and at the same time own nothing. Jesus was quick to point out that His Father cared for His creation, such as flowers, grass, and birds, and would care even more for us, His children (Matt. 6:25–34). In this sense, God promises to meet our needs. Yet, in another sense, Jesus likens His disciples to Himself, as people having no place even to rest their heads (Matt. 8:20). Jesus seems to be saying that we have everything we need in the context of having nothing! It's one of the great, seemingly paradoxical statements with which Jesus confronts us, like "if you lose your life, you'll find it" (Matt. 10:39), or "if you want to lead, you must first be the servant of all" (Matt. 20:26).

The apostle Paul could say that he had learned to be content in any condition because he understood that his wealth was in his relationship with Christ, not in possessions or positions.

In contrast, the American perspective is to acquire wealth, or at least comfort, which is one reason America is in such sad shape today. We do not regard ourselves as vagrants, but as property owners. Being a vagrant contradicts the notion of acquiring things for personal comfort or ownership of those things intrinsic to the successful American lifestyle. Paul emphasized that having little or much money isn't what makes one rich or poor. Rather, it's the degree to which we conform to Jesus and understand that God will honor those who recognize that all they own is God's to use for His purposes. Jesus' definition of poverty was not about one's material or economic condition, but about one's mindset. Anything we value more highly than obedience to Him is a distraction. In this sense, ownership of anything is a hindrance—whether material, emotional, or relational—if it supplants our faith in Jesus.

The Incarnation was not just to save people, but to show them a working, walking model of God's definition of His kingdom. Jesus' definition of poverty was radically different from our economic understanding of poverty. He understood that man's satisfaction with himself and his world is best understood in terms of the spirit. Poverty of the spirit is what really keeps people enslaved and is unaffected by material things such as money or position. Being poor materially may keep one less comfortable, but not necessarily less joyful or content. Being rich spiritually gives us the joy, inner peace, and security that everyone strives for, yet cannot achieve with material possessions. Jesus was devoted to communicating a spiritual understanding of our relationship to this world. When we recognize that, we truly have wealth.

In an interview with *Time* magazine, Mother Teresa said, "The more you have, the more you are occupied, the less you give. But the less you have, the more free you are. Poverty for us is freedom. . . . I find the rich much poorer. Sometimes they are more lonely inside. They are never satisfied. They always need something more. . . . I find that poverty hard to remove. The hunger for love is much more difficult to remove than the hunger for bread."[1]

May the vagrant faith spirit of having

everything and owning nothing be a part of your lifestyle.

[1]"A Pencil in the Hand of God." *Time*, December 4, 1989.

4

The Potter and the Clay

Have you ever put the world on hold and stopped to watch a bubbling brook snake its way through a forest, or a stream of cascading water as it plunges to the ground from a waterfall? There's an uncanny attraction to listen attentively, as if expecting the water to begin a conversation. It's so peaceful, tranquil, even mesmerizing. It almost puts you to sleep, as if nature were singing you a lullaby.

Creation speaks a certain language that points to the Master Designer. There's a majesty and awe to it that leaves you spellbound.

The pounding surf is both peaceful and violent, dynamic and calm. The same is true of the bubbling brook or cascading waterfall. God's natural order, best expressed through His creation, is exciting to behold. It speaks clearly, yet at the same time softly. The same should be true of our lives.

Now compare this feeling to the feeling you get when you have a leaky faucet, like the one in my bathroom. Have you ever tried to sleep as the sound of dripping water breaks the silence with its melodic plunk? Its torturous routine can induce insanity.

Similarly, our attempts to communicate our faith in God can resemble either the language of creation or the object of man's invention. Amidst the busyness of your life, in stressful situations, do you put people at ease with your witness, like the pounding surf or the waterfall?

Do people find rest in your presence? Or is your life like the leaky faucet, more closely resembling an irritating presence rather than a peaceful witness?

In Psalm 46:10, God spoke through the psalmist to admonish us to "be still, and know that I am God." God reveals Himself best when we are doing and saying nothing. Since faith comes by *hearing* the Word of God, we must take time to listen to know what God is telling us to do. When we are so caught up in doing things for God, we're usually too busy to hear Him.

God can take our lives, as He does with His creation, and give us peace in the midst of the most stressing situations. In a violent storm, the tree may bend, but it will not break. When that happens, others will sense a strength that only God can provide.

Maybe we can learn something about our place in the world by watching God's creation. Some years ago, I had an opportunity to spend some time with friends at Martha's Vineyard on Cape Cod. The beauty of the surroundings had God's fingerprints all over it and inspired this poem.

O Lord, I thank You for creation and how
    it mirrors Your image.
When we retreat to Your kingdom,
It's not merely to view animals, lakes or
    trees,
But to catch a glimpse of You as You speak
    to us.

O Lord, we see You in the dragonfly as it
    darts to and fro,
and in the ant as it always appears to be in
    a state similar to the
last shopping day before Christmas.
We see You in the spider as it clumsily
    waddles along,
seemingly in all four directions at once!

The dragonfly, the ant and the spider
are all Your creations,
and used by You no matter how unseemly
    or useless they appear.
When will we learn from them
to appreciate who we are?
I wonder if a dragonfly ever wanted to be
    an ant?

O Lord, we see You in the beautiful, clear
    lake
which invites us to swim in its clear, cool
    waters.
And when we leave the lake,
as when we leave Your presence,
we are refreshed.
The lake, too, bears Your image.

O Lord, we see You in the mighty trees
As they point upward toward You.
When You blow on them during a storm,
they know their place in the kingdom,

and bow quietly before You in an attitude
    of respect for Your power.
When will we learn from the tree,
tall and strong and proud,
yet humble enough to bow before its
    Creator when called upon
and not fight back?

O Lord, when will we learn the secrets of
    Your creation?
When will our nature match Yours?

God's creation gives us a picture of the
beauty and serenity available to all His crea-
tures if we would only listen and understand
our part in His sovereign plan.

God's creation versus man's invention.
The score isn't even close.

5

Leap of Faith

If you could emulate any figure in all of human history, who would that be?

I bet many people would answer "Jesus." He most certainly would be high on the list. Whether one considers Him to be God or not, many regard Jesus as the one person in all of human history who most epitomizes the virtues of brotherhood, love, truth, justice, and a host of other qualities that most people consider admirable.

If this is so, why don't more people follow Christ? Apart from the realization that some will always prefer darkness to light, could it be that many would but don't know how?

Could it also be that many don't know how because we've poorly communicated how to make the connection, bridge the gap, or make the leap of faith necessary to know Him?

Paul asks how people can hear if people aren't sent. Better yet, how can people respond if, after they've heard, no one helps them over to the other side?

Sometimes our best efforts to attract unbelievers are pretty unattractive. Many times, in our efforts to lead people into the kingdom, we misrepresent God's message of mercy and grace and leave the impression that the good news is solely that to reject Christ is to spend eternity without God. This is legitimate, but hardly sensitive to the person trying to understand the reality of God in the first place.

I'm sure the next question on a person's mind is, "If that's the good news, then what's the bad news?" That's a pretty good question. Nowhere to go but down from there.

Instead, we need to communicate that God is *so* good, conviction of personal need and sin leads not to imprisonment in some church-bound existence, as some would fear, but to release and to relationships for which people desperately search. The world is waiting to

hear and respond to that message of uncondi-
tional love and to see it in action among the
members of this body of Christ.

The good news is that Christ came to save
sinners (you and me) and help us find the way
back to God because we are incapable of doing so through our own efforts. Paul, in
2 Corinthians 5:18–21, tells us that we are reconcilers, people who are trying to reestablish
friendship between God and man—a friendship
that was once there, but was lost because of sin
and alienation. That's a great vision for our
calling—to encourage those who don't know
God to see Him as their friend and once again
be on speaking terms.

We try desperately to bring unbelievers
over to "our side," so we attempt to build
bridges to span the gap between us and them.
Unfortunately, in building our bridges, we
don't quite complete them. We only go so far to
be involved in their lives, show our love for
them, and communicate that Jesus meets them
right where they are. We stop just short of the
other side and leave them to finish the span.

We then stand on the edge of the unfinished span and scream for people to make the
"leap of faith." A leap of faith is one thing. Hav-

ing to break the record in the running long jump is another. To get there, you have to be a world class athlete! And when the invitation doesn't seem so inviting, the leap takes even more faith!

Many who attempt this acrobatic feat fall short and land in deep water. We throw them a life preserver and tell them to hang on until we can fish them out. Or until God "delivers" them from their predicament. How nice. We throw them trite clichés as life preservers *after* encouraging them to jump in, in the first place. I don't know if I'd want to listen to this advice after such an experience.

The world looks on in amazement at this practice of getting people into the kingdom. They would like to feel that they are welcome on our side, but a half-built bridge doesn't convey that feeling. And having to jump through hoops to make the grade is more like a circus than a church.

Jesus wants us to complete the bridge to the other side. If we do not extend ourselves totally to others in our outreach efforts, we leave the impression that we expect them to measure up to some undefined standard before we'll finally accept them. Or they may get the feeling that our outreach efforts seem more like filling quotas than fulfilling needs, leaving them with the idea that they are merely notches on our spiritual gunhandles.

The whole purpose of building a bridge is so that *either* side can cross over to the other. People can get to you; you can get to them. They need to be able to travel back and forth to see how we live. After accepting the invitation, they should find it easier to make the journey across. If people have access to us, they'll feel more comfortable coming over. Being familiar with the territory takes away much of the trepidation when making such an important decision.

And once they do cross over, new believers don't have to please us, only Jesus. People are looking for realness amid the falseness that surrounds them. Jesus was constantly battling the hypocrisy of religious people who could only relate to others by comparing their faith with another's. While religious leaders set standards, Jesus knew that no standard could please God. That's why He gave us grace. With so little to believe in anymore, Jesus gives us so much in which to trust. People can respect Jesus because He completed bridges all the way to the

LIGHTHOUSE
Christian Supplies

Close Out Sale

Convent Glen Shopping Centre
6477 Jeanne D Arc Blvd
Orleans, Ontario

Bibles, Books, Cards,
Christian Music, Gifts,
T-Shirts, Games,
Confirmation & First
Communion Products

4 Days Only

April 14 - 17

837-6783

30 - 90% off Entire Stock

other side. And to the worst section of town, where tax collectors, prostitutes, and lepers lived.

So when talking to your neighbor or a friend at the office, remember to finish building the extra section of the bridge, free of toll barriers, so that when they come over to see what it's like in our land, they'll want to stay. Many people are honestly looking for a way over to the side that makes the most sense.

6

When the Perfect Comes

"But when that which is perfect has come, then that which is in part will be done away. . . . For now we see in a mirror dimly, but then face to face . . ." (1 Cor. 13:10, 12).

Within the body of Christ, there are always those who want to "help" God with His job responsibilities. Some would even claim that when Paul said we see through a glass dimly, he meant that the glass was dirty and in need of Windex. And we're right there with washcloth and soap in hand to help God clean up, busy scrubbing away the dirt in our lives that clouds our perception of what it is to live the Christian life.

As a result, we spend our time attempting to impress God and others by trying to clean the glass as much as possible, hoping to see more clearly what it is God wants us to do. If we can see more clearly, we think, then maybe we can understand more about ourselves and become better Christians—which leads to being a more perfect believer.

I think we have it all wrong.

Paul expressed it best when he said in 2 Corinthians 12:9 that "My grace is sufficient for you, for My strength is made perfect in weakness." Paul knew that his ability to understand God's working in his life was like looking through a glass dimly. His information was partial. No matter how hard he tried to put aside his imperfection, pray it away or overcome it, ultimately, it would be instrumental in his service to God. He wasn't busy trying to clean the glass to see more closely, but rather, to follow more closely what he saw clearly already.

Still, we vainly attempt to clean ourselves up in order to live the Christian life. As a result, our service to God becomes a legalistic, selfish pursuit. Thankfully, those verses in 1 Corinthians 13 tell me just the opposite— that everything I need to know about living the Christian life will only make sense when I stand before God. Until then, let me follow what I can see clearly: the person of Jesus.

The apostle John says in 1 John 4:8 that God is love. He does not say God is faith or works or hope. That's because true communion with God leads to love, which is at the heart of every true relationship. Paul stresses the concept of love so much in 1 Corinthians 13 because it is the overriding identification of the believer, the one thing that comes closest to resembling godly behavior—more than our knowledge, our unique gifts and talents, or even great faith.

Without love, Paul says, I become sounding brass or a clanging cymbal (1 Cor. 13:1). He emphasizes that love wins out over everything else, including imperfection; God's love extends to us through Christ, and our love extends horizontally to others in Christ's name. When I see that, I understand that love is a total commitment to an imperfect person. This is illustrated best in God's grace working through Jesus to assure us of our salvation.

Paul understood that his goal was not to become perfect, but to become more loving. He infers that one needn't have all knowledge or be perfect to see Christ, just have a ready and loving heart for God. Understanding this allows me to accept that my imperfection will not prevent me from seeing Christ. Rather, the Bible is clear that my imperfection should drive me *to* Christ because I realize my need for a Savior.

Many Christians strive for perfection in their "spiritual walk" at the expense of love to achieve good marks, as if God were keeping a report card on them. Trying to achieve perfection keeps us bound up doing things to gain God's approval and give meaning to our Christian experience. But the Bible states emphatically that imperfection is really the norm because the gospel is for those who are imperfect. Paul's assurance of seeing Christ face to face was based on God's promise, not on his ability to please God. "Now, I'm imperfect; then, I will be perfect," he says. Regardless of how good I think I am, I will never be able to achieve perfection because my ability to do so is inherently limited.

Still, in spite of what Paul is telling us, we continue to surge full steam ahead to do as much as we can, believing that our faith rests in what we've done for God lately, not what God has done with us lately. Quite a difference by comparison.

This mindset among Christians of working toward perfection is a type of manic-myopia, a pathological form of tunnel vision resulting in limited ability to see the full dimension of God's Word. We are bent on heading in only one direction. We do not realize that there are other roads for us to use if we would just look around. We're too busy staying on the one road we like, trying desperately to get others to travel that same road, because we think it's the only road worth taking.

We don't need a better picture of what God wants; we have all the picture we need. We just need to spend more time knowing and loving God, not trying to do things or being perfect for Him. That's why the psalmist tells us to be still and know that He is God (Ps. 46:10). Knowing God better and gaining His pleasure are accomplished by being still so that we can hear what He would like us to do.

In God's eyes, perfection is not a measure of performance but of promise—the promise that Christ is perfect. People will be attracted to us by the light of God in us, not the light we try to create by how perfectly we try to be Christians. This frees us to concentrate on the relationship itself, rather than the results of the relationship.

Understanding that freedom is found in our imperfection enables us to be satisfied with who we are and the promise that we look dimly in a glass for now. Trying to clean the glass only gets us a better look at ourselves, not a better look at God.

Put down the Windex. The glass will not get any cleaner with all your efforts. Instead, be still and know that God wants you as you are. If you can do this, people won't have to look at you and wonder how they can measure up. Instead, they'll see imperfection and know that there's hope for them too.

7

School of Interior Design

Have you ever had the opportunity to build your own house?

I never have. But I always imagined what it would be like to work with an architect to design my own place. I dreamed of the chance to take each room, empty and unfinished, and fix it to reflect my own style and taste. I could really do it right!

As I thought about that, 1 Corinthians 6:19 came to mind: "Do you not know that your body is the temple of the Holy Spirit who is in you, whom you have from God, and you are not your own?" Paul describes our bodies as temples in which God chooses to reside. I wondered if God's desire to custom build in me a unique housing for Himself was at all similar to my dream of designing a home.

In order to explore this from another perspective, I subscribed to *Ageless Architect,* the publication for those who want to remodel their worn-out, run-down homes. After looking through this publication, I knew that it really wasn't for the do-it-yourselfers. It called for custom designs by one company—The Grand Designer. It has offices everywhere. Pretty expensive, I would suspect.

First of all, it specializes in renovating *old homes,* not building new ones. It takes dilapidated buildings and refurbishes them completely. The renovation includes a great deal of retrofitting to restore the former beauty of the house: some fresh paint, stripping away old paint to reveal beautiful woodwork, patching up walls, shoring up the foundation, adding new furniture that goes with the style of the house. The transformation is amazing; you wouldn't know it was the same place!

The result? A once uninhabitable house becomes a much sought-after residence. The craftsmanship, particularly the inside work, is impressive enough to attract any potential buyer!

That's what happens when we live the Christian life. We find in God a Grand Designer who provides quality renovation of worn out temples. When Christ is allowed to be the designer (the author and finisher of our faith), He coordinates every aspect of the design. As a result, everything about us—our personalities, lifestyles, work, and personal habits—fits together and is attractive and appealing. As a result, people will be so impressed with the renovation, they will flock to the Designer and Architect.

I'm afraid that, though God wants complete control of the decorating, many of us prefer the do-it-yourself, start-from-scratch method.

The do-it-yourselfer is often inconsistent and incomplete in his method of building his home. Sometimes, he only concentrates on the outside. He can build a new home to look like a Beverly Hills postcard: great architecture, perfectly manicured lawn, a pool and jacuzzi too. But one thing is missing in this spectacular house—the inside! Sort of reminds me of a Hollywood set. On one side, a set could look like the Taj Mahal. On the other, three wooden posts prop up this one-dimensional piece. It certainly isn't what it appears to be! Neither are we sometimes. Like many lives today, the inside of the house is empty. We concentrate on improving the outside, while neglecting the inside. We're more concerned about making a good impression with what is immediately visible than with spending the effort on the inside, where the changes are not as noticeable and fewer people are likely to see. We have no desire to have Christ renovate our interior lives.

Sometimes the do-it-yourselfers forsake the outside to concentrate on the inside only. They prefer their own decorating, thinking they have a better handle on what belongs there and how it will look. But their idea of decorating is simply to rearrange the furniture, which is a far cry from the designer look Christ has promised. This "furniture" can be Bible reading, praying, or witnessing. These are important to the overall look, but that's all they concentrate on. Sometimes, the furniture is more valued than the One who enabled us to have it. A room with just the furniture and no appropriate wallpaper, window treatments, or paintings to enhance the overall design lacks the beauty, style, and warmth brought to a room uniquely arranged by the Grand Designer's custom look.

Sometimes the do-it-yourselfer will try to save a little money and take certain designs that look good in one house and try to apply them to his house. He thinks they'll work equally as well. Why spend extra for a custom design? And the wait is longer too. He can skip the heavy price tag of Christ's involvement; it's cheaper and faster without bringing Him in. But saving money only helps in the short term. Ultimately, the house will fall apart if he builds this way. The materials Christ uses when building and renovating will last forever.

Whether they're working on the outside or inside, the do-it-yourselfers are also always decorating yet never finishing. There's always so much work to be done. "It'll get done in time," they say. But that time never comes. Instead, the outside never resembles that Hollywood set and, on the inside, many of the rooms remain half finished, all because the decorators want to be in control. And a half finished room can look worse than a neatly kept empty room.

Ultimately, there's no sense in skimping.

Christ Himself is necessary to the overall design. The more we furnish our house with His presence, and not just the things His presence should bring, the more valuable our homes become. When was the last time you had a spiritual appraisal of your house? It would be nice to see how much you're worth on the current real estate market.

If you're in need of an interior decorator, call for the One who will custom design your temple. He makes house calls at no extra charge. One word of caution: If you decide to use His services, follow His recommendations. The value of your home will appreciate throughout eternity. What an investment!

8

Play Ball!

Ever wanted to drop all your responsibilities and just get away from it all? Your job, your commitments, even your "faith" and say "I quit"? At times, I feel that way. All I ever wanted to do was to play centerfield for the Yanks. So, when things seem a bit out of control, I yearn to pick up my glove and spikes and head for the stadium.

Life does that to us sometimes. We seem out of touch with God when we feel like our faith isn't really ours. We're desperate for a faith of our own, but it feels as if we're playing in someone else's game by someone else's rules, and expected to live up to someone else's standard too. No one ever really explained the ground rules at the beginning. All we cared about was getting on the team. We'd do anything to "make" the team—even change our batting stance to imitate the top hitter.

When this happens, we know something's wrong. An alarm goes off within us. Danger! Danger! This warning signal is the result of a life of unrealized expectation. There's something more to our life and to our relationship with God, but we can't put our finger on it. What's wrong?

In a natural sense, since God is creative and we are made in His image, to be really fulfilled, people must also be creative. But the notion of creativity isn't solely having artistic ability, for example, or doing things others cannot. It carries the idea of originality, like the snowflake or a fingerprint.

The same applies to our faith. There is nothing less creative or more boring than a secondhand faith. And God cannot work in that environment since He is the God of the original. Our faith must be ours uniquely, expressed in the manner we find most comfortable. Communicating with our Creator is one of the most creative and original actions we can take. Without our own faith, we feel lonely, undeveloped, and out of sync with the world.

Living out a faith defined by someone else's standard settles us into the life of an amateur believer. To the amateur believer, his faith is a challenge, yes, but is not taken very seriously since it is not his livelihood. There's not as much pressure as in the professional ranks, but not as much excitement either. Not as many worries or concerns, but neither is there much fulfillment. Being an amateur Christian has little to offer in the way of real rewards. Too often, we settle for being an amateur when we really should be swinging away as a professional in the big leagues. This amateur lifestyle breeds boredom and a lack of fulfillment, and is the ultimate in lack of creativity. In this context, our faith is not much fun.

We feel out of control when our faith is a copy of someone else's. As a result, our performance on the field as a Christian begins to slip. Our average takes a dive, our fielding becomes sloppy, and the errors mount. Before too long, we're relegated to the bench. Or even worse, we get sent down to the minor leagues. Our faith (which was not really "ours" at all) begins to erode. What was supposed to be fun is now a drag. The game has lost its luster. Defeatism sets in. We even begin to doubt that we'll ever make the team again. That's even more frightening.

So what can we do?

First, get off the merry-go-round. We cannot be content just going along for the ride, with no direction to our lives, or moving from one person's faith to another without having a faith of our own. Ultimately, we won't get too far if we're going in circles.

Second, let Jesus be the model for your faith, not your church or your friends or your denomination. Since He is the only one who can live the Christian life, He must have control of your life. Don't live your life through anyone but Jesus. Only He can make you distinct in a world where everyone competes to be the same. Jesus' distinct relationship with God always confounded the religious leaders. They didn't expect Jesus' answers, or His actions at times. His responses to the woman caught in adultery, paying taxes to the Roman government, or eating at the house of Zacchaeus (a known sinner simply because he was a tax collector), caught the religious folks off balance. They had lost their creativity and originality because their faith and their lives had become a set of rules with no freedom or latitude. They were acting like professionals, but had long been amateurs in their relationships with God.

Thankfully, a personal God yearns to walk with us along the creative path, one designed exclusively for us. Otherwise, we take early retirement, settle for the life of an amateur, or slip into our own dream world.

I can see myself now, running with my back to home plate. It would've been a great catch.

9

No Womb
at the Top

An existentialist writer once said that life is absurd. He must have lived in New York City. "If you can make it in New York, you can make it anywhere," people say. Everyone there is trying to get to the top—climbing, crawling, scraping. They'll do anything just to stay alive and reach the pinnacle before someone else gets there.

But staying at the top after they get there is another thing entirely.

Daily headlines scream at us from their front page podiums telling us of the difficulties of this pursuit. A young woman jogger, viciously attacked by a gang of youths, fights for her life in an intensive care unit; innocent children at play are caught in the crossfire of gun battles between rival drug dealers; politicians and Wall Street kingpins fall to corruption and scandal.

But, I know a place that's become even tougher to make it than New York City: the womb.

Pro-life vs. pro-choice. The debate has moved from the courts to the streets. When life begins is not the issue, some say; personal rights are. But does a person's right to his or her own body extend beyond that body to another, whether an innocent person jogging in the park or an unborn human being? And if people have rights over their own bodies, why do we have laws against suicide or self-inflicted wounds?

The real issue is not rights, but meaningful life. With Christ, life has meaning. And He transforms lives for eternity. The Bible says that God has known us from the beginning of time. His presence is with us from the womb to death and beyond. *God never allows for a disturbance in that continuum.* Neither should we.

What has happened to cause us to devalue life? Everything in our society today is expensive. Only life is cheap. Leaving the gold standard may have devalued our currency; leaving biblical standards has devalued our lives. Ironically, the gang who attacks the woman faces conviction by the same court system that upholds laws to help others take the life of a baby. A voice cries through the ages to give meaning to life—from life in the womb (Ps. 139) to life eternal (1 John 5:11). We place little value on the life we see, even less on the life we can't see. Life after death, life before life; neither holds great meaning for us.

Can it be that the denial of life in the womb is one reason for the decline in meaningful life outside the womb? We've become a generation of anonymous people, lost in ratings, circulation figures, social security numbers, and political bureaucracies that exist to be self-serving rather than serving others. We've become statistics. And statistics have no names or faces. They're easier to say no to, steal from, beat up, even kill.

Christians have an important role in society: to reach into those lives left vacant and devalued by society and to tell them about the

One who can fill their empty hearts with identity and meaning. Christ's standard gives value and meaning to life both inside *and* outside the womb.

The existentialist writer was wrong. Life isn't absurd. *We* are, especially when we try to live life without Christ. With Him, there is plenty of womb at the top.

PART
THREE

A Renewed Mind

"To be made new in the attitude of your minds" (Eph. 4:23).

1

The March of the Trojan Horses

I always liked ancient history, especially read-ing about military campaigns. The Pel-oponnesian Wars, Hannibal's sixteen years in Italy, Caesar's Gallic Wars. You really had to be a strategist to win wars in those days. No launching missiles from a hundred miles away or dropping bombs from an airplane.

One of my favorite stories involved the use of the Trojan Horse. Now that was smart. It sure saved a lot of fighting to get into the city. Imagine, getting your enemy to think he's get-ting a gift when he's really letting in that which will ultimately defeat him. How neat. And how deadly.

In this generation, I get the feeling that history is repeating itself.

We've seen great advancements and developments in science and technology. But with the advancements have come moments of decline. It's like the old saying "I'm not so concerned with where man descended from but rather what he's descending to." Evolution seems to go in both directions.

Certain influences have been so subtle, so cloaked in popular causes, that we have failed to recognize them for what they are. The enemy is not obvious; they've come as wolves in sheep's clothing. There are no invading barbarian hordes, no wild-eyed reprobates lurking behind every corner curling their mustaches in nervous energy. And because we have not seen them for what they are, we've readily embraced these influences as the answers to our problems. Or as Trojan horses. They look like gifts, but once we let them into our gates, we are attacked.

In the name of developing new family models for the future, many voices now advocate single parenting, homosexual parents, and children being reared by surrogate parents. This is disturbing, not so much because it challenges the traditional structure of family life, but because it disregards the concept of the nuclear family as the glue that bonds people and society together. It is this family concept that provides the necessary love, emotional support, and shelter individuals need to function best. Any deviation from that model causes chaos. The family under attack, though, is just one example.

Other popular causes have fostered new displays of personal freedom, bringing rights with no responsibilities, and have become umbrella opportunities for abortion on demand and free speech that denigrates. Winning at any cost in the name of sport, consumerism in the name of economic freedom, and New Age self-worship in the name of religion are all part of a declining cultural trend that sacrifices order and reason to perpetuate our lifestyles and seeks to replace God's creation with our own. You and I now have the chance to be gods too. That's real democracy because if we can be gods, then we're just the kind of gods America deserves.

So beware of our culture bearing gifts.

Waiting outside the gates of our minds are nicely wrapped packages with beautifully inscribed greeting cards. We must watch what we allow into our houses. We must be aware of what is filtering into our redeemed minds. Certain messages constantly wear away at our beliefs, values, and lifestyles. In order to prevent this erosion, we must come to grips with Paul's admonition in Romans 12:2 to renew our minds with that which is pleasing to God. Otherwise, when we least expect it, the trap door will open and down will climb the forces to overtake us while we sleep.

Check around your house today. See any Trojan horses? You might want to return them instead of letting them inside.

2

The Kingdom
of Goods

*S*eek ye first the kingdom of goods because
all things are yours (somewhere in the
Bible).

A certain segment of the church today per-
petuates a disturbing concept that confuses
many people, including me. It's supposed to
make me comfortable in my physical being. Instead, it makes me uncomfortable in my spirit.
It's the notion that the kingdom of God is set
up to satisfy my desires. I don't give up anything; I just receive. I don't give; I get. I'm more

consumed with myself and my needs than with others and their needs.

This attitude has God on call all day. Just dial the right number and He answers immediately. If He's not in, just leave a message on His answering machine and He'll get right back to you.

In contrast, the apostle Paul states in Philippians 4 that he learned to be content in whatever state he found himself, *so that God's agenda would be maximized.* His sole desire was to serve God, regardless of circumstances. He understood that God's sovereignty, not circumstances, dictated the growth of the kingdom. Once he came to that conclusion, God was free to move through him unhindered. He was not caught up with his surroundings, but only with his God. That's what brought peace to his heart and mind then. That's what will bring peace to us today.

To say that God's will for anyone is maximized through only one condition (whether it's abundance or poverty) actually limits God, rather than expressing a limitless God. Paul said in Philippians 4:12 that he got along in both humble and prosperous circumstances—

and everything in between—because his focus was on Christ's strength regardless of the circumstances. He echoed his greatest words of freedom while in chains, his most eloquent example of power when confined with the powerless. What he had was worth more than all the gold in the Roman Empire, though its value could not be counted, measured, or traded.

To say that God only wants abundance or prosperity for us is to fall into the trap of the American mindset that more is best and that best communicates the ultimate good. In America, we're supposed to have a chicken in every pot and two cars in every garage. If that's true, then a Christian living in America ought to have at least that, and probably more, since God wants us to have an abundant life. Right? Abundant life is a funny thing, though. Abundance to one is poverty to another. And poverty to one is abundance to another. In this sense, the parameters of legitimate expressions of Christian living are defined in the context of the American dream. This is an illusion.

In fact, there are no parameters to an infinite God who does as He pleases to accomplish His will in our lives, using poverty and wealth and everything in between to achieve that end. To claim that God wants anything for us, materially or otherwise, other than conformity to His Son, is to misunderstand God. But it's easy to misunderstand God, particularly in our culture. We confuse what we want, living in America, with what God wants for us living in the world.

We tend to look at God's will and Word through the filter of the American dream. This makes Christianity more palatable to many Americans, so that it might become more acceptable, so that it might be embraced more readily, so that we can be more comfortable this side of heaven. Should I buy the whole package now, or put it on installments on my credit card?

To conform to the American dream of security, abundance, and possessions, we have come up with a parallel American Christian dream, a new kind of kingdom living that's in stark contrast to the example of Paul in Philippians. We have created a kingdom of goods, a self-serving Christianity, devoid of spiritual struggle or sacrifice, or identification with the broken, and one which promises great rewards as your birthright. Sounds real American to me. In this sense, the kingdom of goods stands right alongside the Magic Kingdom.

It's the American dream. But a nightmare to God.

3

New Age or Ice Age?

A bout twelve years ago, a friend invited me to a seminar in a New York City hotel which turned out to be an introduction to *est*. The room was filled to capacity with neat, good-looking New York City types—very chic and yuppie.

As a journalist, and as a Christian, I wanted to hear and see what went on at one of these meetings; what the attraction was that brought these people together. Would anything said parallel Scripture and would this room full of seekers respond to the invitation to find out more about *est?*

My friend and I had spoken often about the claims of Christ. He was struggling with the way to interpret these claims in light of his life-style: raising a family, meeting his bills with a struggling business that left him just enough at the end of the month, and trying to find meaning in a mundane life.

As I walked into the room and looked for a seat, I wondered if all these people were here to seek an answer to a spiritual quest, or if they were just curious. I would soon find out.

As the meeting started, two very bright, attractive people came out on stage. The woman began by thanking everyone for attending something that would change their lives and proceeded to familiarize people with their surroundings and others by having people in one section of the room wave to another section, and so on. It was a great way to melt the ice and build cohesion among strangers. A nice touch, I thought. She must have received an A in group dynamics.

As the night wore on, we were fed the usual rhetoric of how we could better ourselves through implementing the *est* philosophy and how life could be so much more meaningful. I remember going to the men's room during the break where someone asked me how I was. I responded in my usual matter-of-fact, confident manner, with a smile, that life was good, thank you. His immediate response was, "Oh, you must have taken the training."

I nodded and smiled to myself as I walked away.

What training?

The night wore on, and I was getting tired of this guy telling me that by taking the training, I could receive information that would change my life. They even had testimonies of people who were changed through "the training." Of course, they never really got to the training. To get that, one would have to plunk down $350 for a weekend. Of course.

As I left that night with my friend, I realized that in spite of all the friendliness and exuberance, people still seemed distant. Everyone was pumped during the session, really into themselves and the speaker. And then it was over. Afterward, everyone went right back to their "faces," as if a switch went on and off. The self-help movement without the Spirit of God may be helpful for a moment, but not for eternity.

The good news is that there's a growing desire in our land to search for and experience spiritual meaning in our lives. The bad news is that Jesus isn't the One people are finding to help fulfill that desire.

Instead, people are listening to leaders who tell them to turn inward to find direction and meaning. People are giving up thinking for themselves and are beginning to think only of themselves. This is a far cry from Paul's admonition in Philippians 2:3–4 to, look not only to your own interests, but also to the interests of others.

The more we seek to find fulfillment from within, the more we must deal with ourselves. What a horrible preoccupation. It's like trying to get water from an empty well: A lot of work goes into getting to the point where we come up empty. Once we've finished and discovered the emptiness, we still struggle to find some meaning for all our effort.

Ultimately, we must look for some meaning in the search itself since there's none at the conclusion. The result of all this activity has created a society of spiritual thrill seekers who are trying to feel better about what they've discovered about themselves. They must focus on self-improvement, always searching for self-understanding and the space and freedom to gain this understanding. The water must be down there somewhere, they say.

The term *new age* has been applied to this movement, and to other seemingly related aspects of this experience, everything from soft music, to a certain cuisine, to a line of clothing. New age thinking forfeits the future for the present. It's designed to provide a better life-style—for me. But that's the problem: me.

New age thinking is not about the kingdom of God. It's about the kingdom of Self. New age spirituality creates anonymity as people become obsessed with self and disassociated from others. Caring for others is not in the formula. One can only care for oneself.

The key word in all this "new wave" of the spirit is *cold*. In reality, the new age will be just another ice age unless we tell people about Jesus' plan for self-improvement. In contrast, Jesus points out that seeking after self-improvement begins only when we let go of our life. "He who loves his life will lose it, and he who hates his life in this world will keep it for eternal life" (John 12:25) and, "I am the vine, you are the branches. He who abides in Me, and I in him, bears much fruit; for without Me you can do nothing" (John 15:5).

Jesus' plan is so much easier and more truthful. When He grabs hold of your life, you'll never be the same—not only for yourself, but for everyone who comes into contact with you. In Romans 8:6, Paul says that the mind controlled by the Spirit is life and peace. He continues in 12:2 to affirm that the renewing of our minds proves what the will of God is in our lives, that which is good, acceptable, and perfect.

With a renewed mind, we can have a new perspective on life that permeates every aspect of our thoughts and actions. Now that's good news for anyone looking for self-improvement.

By the way, my friend never did follow through with the *est* training. Jesus was much more practical.

4

Escapism—A Nice Place to Visit

Our world is rapidly changing before our very eyes. The pace is dizzying. Significant events occur daily. Lifestyle patterns develop quicker than we can comprehend. We're living a sort of time-lapse life; everything's so fast, even in slow motion.

This cultural environment has resulted in the relinquishing of the responsibility of decision-making corporately (which has left huge gaps in government and business ethics), and personally (leaving gaps in personal relationships and an increase in substance abuse), and has become fertile ground in which the seeds of escapism can flourish.

Escapism as a lifestyle occurs when certain influences on our perception of reality condition us to believe that the available choices for our lives are no longer valid or attainable because of a changing, and often hostile, world.

Former reference points by which we defined, evaluated, and chartered meaningful lifestyles have been either clouded or replaced by new reference points that do not adequately answer the important questions about mankind's existence: his purpose, direction, and the search for inner peace. In the past, it didn't matter if every person believed the Bible literally. Reference points from a biblical base advocating certain standards and ethics to achieve stability were generally accepted, and offered direction and purpose to life. In recent years, the decline of the biblical base has rendered the "old ways" useless in society's eyes. Yet, the new ways (i.e., humanism, relativism, rampant secularism) have not fulfilled us, either. As a result, humans feel trapped and desperately search for a way out of this predicament. Hence, the need to escape.

Escapism has brought with it a surge of introspection, characterized most by an increase in spiritual awareness. A host of new age religions have sprung up in response to the pressing need in the human heart for answers beyond oneself.

Amidst this wave of searching, Christians have a golden opportunity to chart the road to meaningful life for those who no longer have any reference points in theirs. As they look to escape their predicaments, our lives should be their escape routes. Unfortunately, a form of escapism has also infiltrated our churches and Christian institutions. We've retreated from the world, not only geographically, but emotionally through prayer meetings, church work, self-righteous crusades, and a host of other works and attitudes that deny the reference point of allowing Christ to be one's all in all. In the process, we've left the uniquely Christian aspects of who we are: caretakers of the hungry and the homeless, the poor and the oppressed; upholders of integrity and honor and fidelity in marriage and relationships.

Christians have abdicated their real power base in the world in order to create a separate world—one in which they can remain untouched by the neighbor in need, the AIDS victim, and the person in the next pew who may not be exactly our choice of the model churchgoer. We keep our distance from this new class of untouchables so as to be untainted and unaffected.

Thus, the sign posts which identified Christians have been torn down and replaced by ones unattractive to the nonbeliever, who now has to look elsewhere for his reference points. Unfortunately, the reference points that are foundational to biblical lifestyles are also foundational in society. Lose sight of those and nothing significant remains.

Jesus was so right when He said that we would change the world only through our involvement in it, not isolation from it: when we are like the good Samaritan and care for the person who society and religious folks would be least likely to help; when we seek to be less spiritual and more loving. He told us to be salt and light in the world. Instead, we've abandoned the Christian worldview of reconciliation and going the extra mile for a worldview that says we needn't deal with the problems. We've become self-indulgent rather than self-denying.

We've exchanged realness for a hollow holiness. Unbelievers couldn't care less about how holy we are but more about how real we are. There are few stumbling blocks for the unbeliever, but many to the self-righteous. People are not looking for a rule for living, but a reason for living—for unreal love in a real world.

In an increasingly self-serving society, the only way they will find this kind of love is for Christians to return to the land and build, like Nehemiah did, regardless of the apparent harsh circumstances and hostile environment. Then people will know that God is indeed in charge of the operation, and say, "for they perceived that this work was done by our God" (Neh. 6:16). No need to escape anymore when we find a world that is real.

5

Pew-Trified

Be honest now. How often do you sit in church looking as if you were absolutely spellbound by the message when really you were daydreaming? Or sleeping with your eyes open? Many times your sole Christian experience is to attend church each week. You have no active involvement in the life of the church, whether corporately or personally, and no emotion or desire to become involved in another person's life. Just show up, do your time, and leave. Sort of like going to work, punching the clock, and receiving a weekly paycheck. To you, the payoff in the Christian life is a place in heaven. But for now, you must do time down here.

Strangely, when viewed in those terms, your Christian experience more closely resembles a prison sentence than the abundant life Jesus promised. Over an extended period of time, this attitude leads to hardening of your spiritual arteries—blocking the flow of the Holy Spirit in your life and creating an almost irreversible state of indifference to restoring spiritual health. You may be a warm body in the pew, but you're spiritually dead. The perfect environment is now created for pew-trification to set in.

A church full of these individuals resembles the Petrified Forest: the natural phenomenon where living organisms (specifically trees) died ages ago, but have been preserved by some miracle of nature. Looks good on the outside but is really dead on the inside. And hardened beyond belief.

Many of us, like those trees, are petrified too. There's nothing alive about us. We sit in pews on Sunday like dead trees. And not only does hardness set in as we stay there, but a certain aroma emanates from us.

Second Corinthians 2:15–16 says a Christian is to God the "fragrance of Christ among those who are being saved and among those who are perishing. To the one we are the aroma of death leading to death, and to the other the aroma of life leading to life." The aroma of death is the unique smell of the *pew-trified Christian;* a believer who has been petrified in the pew and is of no use to God. Something I once read from Francis Schaeffer has been a constant reminder of the end result of the pew-trified Christian. He said, "The Christian must resist the spirit of the world in the form it takes in his generation. He must understand what confronts him antagonistically in his moment in history. . . . Otherwise, he simply becomes a museum piece, and not a living warrior for Christ."

For the most part, a museum piece sits on a shelf and collects dust. When people walk past, they remark how relevant it was to the past, but that it has little or no relevance to their world today. In reality, it's an expensive relic.

One of my greatest concerns is that I would become a museum piece or a pew-trified

Christian. As a believer, my life must count for something. If not, going to church will not give me life, only a seat in a building.

James 1:22 admonishes us to be doers of the Word, not just hearers. We cannot be content to merely occupy a position in a pew and call that worship; we must experience a tangible expression of God working in our lives. And our doing is a tangible expression of His work. A tree that's alive will bear fruit. That's being a doer. A pew-trified tree bears no fruit because it's dead. That's being a hearer.

Ideally, the church is a place for dead people to find life, not for dead people who want to remain dead. It's the place where once-dead, twice-born people can live anew as Christ's ambassadors and reconcilers (2 Cor. 5:18–21).

Next time you're in church, take a look around. See anyone looking a bit pew-trified? How about yourself? If so, it's time for a new work environment and a spiritual check-up to unclog those blocked arteries before your heart hardens to the point that nothing can take root.

The road to recovery may take a while. But in the end, not only you, but others will notice a different fragrance in your life. The hardness of the pew-trified person will give way to the softness of the Spirit. If not checked, you may become just a relic of the past with no life to share with anyone.

If our lives are like this, non-Christians won't be able to see the forest because of the trees. The pew-trified ones.

6

Let Us Make Man . . .

The headlines are becoming more and more frightening. Crack dealers terrorize neighborhoods, hate crimes terrorize the innocent, and homeless people—nomads in the deserts of urban landscapes—terrorize the American conscience.

We look for answers to these dilemmas or for someone to blame, yet we continually ignore the fact that one result of an increasingly secular society is a disturbing new perspective of the image of mankind. This perspective has contributed, more than anything else, to our society's lost identity. And lost people.

We have exchanged the concept of man made in the image of God with man made in the image of whatever direction our culture wants to go. It's designed to reflect the times, and our own desires. Distorting the biblical model of mankind and our relationship to a personal Creator is a dangerous precedent.

Previously, the biblical model elevated people to a position of immeasurable worth, so that when conveyed horizontally to others, it provided a national conscience that cared for the destitute and saw through the blindness of hate. It was a glue which held society together for the common good.

Today, the common good is very uncommon.

Over the past generation, that biblical concept has been eroded. People are now seen as utilitarian, and as such, are only as good as their last achievement. This lessens a person's view of self, and thus, dehumanizes him or her. The results of this dehumanization is a society characterized by anonymity. And we've created not only an anonymous society, but a heartless one.

This growing anonymity has exacerbated the homeless situation. Homeless people remain inconspicuous because they've lost their usefulness to a society that no longer recognizes its responsibility to care.

People have been translated into ratings shares for a consumer-oriented society. They are outlets for products—cogs in the wheels of Madison Avenue marketers. Not people made in the image of God.

The purpose is to create humans in a marketable image which is representative of many mindsets and choices. An image for everyone.

Many times, though, there's no real need for a product. But that's no problem. With the right kind of advertising, we can create a need. Put it out there and see how many flock to it. Illusions are created daily. And bought by many.

People are no longer affirmed in their simple humanity; we strive to be something we aren't, to live up to something that's not real.

We'd expect that from the world, but not from the church. But it's happening there too.

We look to "evangelize" people who are from our social status, who are more attractive, who will be able to give more. We look for those who conform to an image, instead of those who express a need for God, or who represent those with whom we'd like least to fellowship.

Another intrusion into our redeemed minds is the notion of deviancy. Not only have we been told that we must do something, act in some manner, or buy something to be loved, accepted, and successful, we are taken one step further to depend on the approval of others as the measure of our worth and identity. It's no longer good enough to be accepted by Jesus; it helps if the church accepts me too.

This is disastrous. It distorts reality by creating the perception that if ugliness in a person exists, it is deviant. We no longer see ourselves as God sees us. Nothing is ever said about those whom the world deems ugly but God deems beautiful.

Subliminally or otherwise, we have been influenced by the message that our acceptance becomes a condition of wearing the right clothes and using the right deodorant and mouthwash.

As long as we continue to elevate the wrong concepts of meaningful life and the intrinsic worth of the individual, we'll continue to have a neurotic society . . . and a neurotic church.

The church is the only institution which can rehumanize society because it still has the right image to follow. It's Jesus: the same yesterday, today, and forever.

7

Pickpockets of Peace

In 1988, the front page headlines in New York were as stark as the weather—an earthquake in Soviet Armenia killed tens of thousands. Many more were left homeless and succumbed to the cold, unable to be helped by the Soviet bureaucracy. How could that happen?

At the same time, in one day, three homeless men in New York died of exposure to the cold. Ironically, their iron grate deathbeds were in the shadows of Tiffany's, Trump Tower, and Bloomingdale's—*and* Gracie Mansion, home of the mayor. Once again, a government bureaucracy was unable to help.

The circumstances were worlds apart; the results, strikingly similar. "Is a homeless person any more homeless in Russia than in New York City?" I thought.

The United States rushed in to offer aid to those stricken Soviet citizens. Gorbachev later thanked the United States for its efforts. Only a few days prior to the disaster, during an official visit to the United States, Gorbachev was shaking hands and smiling with people in Times Square.

At the same time, both governments continued to spend billions in defense equipment to oppose each other.

Is this a cold war? Or a cold world?

Peace is a prevalent word in our current vocabulary. The Middle East struggles for an elusive peace treaty between Arabs and Jews. Moslems and Christians still battle each other in Lebanon while the government tries to establish peace. Eastern Europe tries to reassemble itself after tumultuous political upheaval. And the mayor hires more police to guard the streets.

We think peace is obtained by signing treaties, stamping out opposition, shaking hands, and forcing politically advantageous smiles while posing for pictures.

All this posturing reminds me of an old television program called "Racket Squad," which chronicled the efforts of a particular arm of the law that apprehended con artists. The star of the program, Reed Hadley, would always come on after the show and leave viewers with this bit of sage advice: "Remember, there are people who can pat you on the back with one hand and pick your pocket with the other." When I read and hear of certain attempts at peace by our president and some of our "allies," I feel as if Reed Hadley is speaking to me. We're patting each other on the back while we put our hands in each other's pockets.

Above all the rhetoric of government propaganda, one thing stands out. The cold war did not originate as a battle between democracy and communism. It started with you and me, husband and wife, black and white. People stop talking with one another, working with each other, trusting each other, believing in each other. The same process can kill a relationship between two people or two countries.

Cold wars begin with cold hearts. And

cold hearts develop whenever we fail to abide by Jesus' command to love each other as we love ourselves. The apostle Paul outlined this attitude in Philippians 2:3–4: "Let nothing be done through selfish ambition or conceit, but in lowliness of mind let each esteem others better than himself. Let each of you look out not only for his own interests, but also for the interests of others." If practiced, the words of Jesus and Paul would have forestalled many a broken relationship or broken ties between countries.

The U.N. may define peace as the absence of guns and war. But, in fact, peace is the absence of conflict in the human heart. And only Jesus can change a heart. If He could address the issue of peace at the United Nations, He would talk about individual transformation, not world politics. And Jesus does speak—every day.

You and I have an opportunity to live as the Jesus of Matthew 25, to be His voice and face. Perhaps we need to have our perspective broadened to understand the unique ways we can reach into a person's heart with the message of the Gospel, and touch it with God's love. In the midst of earthquakes and debates about homeless people and homeland rule, the world best understands and accepts Jesus when he comes as described in Matthew 25—as one with a cup of water, a shelter for the dispossessed, clothing for the naked, or as a visitor to the prisoner. And in New York, incarceration is not confined to a cell on Rikers Island. It can be in a penthouse at the Waldorf or at a corner table at the 21 Club.

We must point to and represent the One who can feed the hungry, give hope in the midst of trying circumstances, raise the dead, and promise eternal life. We can't wait for governments to help. That road is strewn with futile efforts.

Contrary to world opinion, the seats of power do not exist in Washington or Moscow. They're located in my heart. And in your heart. And each day of our lives, Jesus calls us to the conference table to settle our own cold wars. His definition and quality of peace is unmatched by anything the world can offer (John 14:27).

World peace begins at home when Jesus takes up residence in the true seat of power. When that happens, fear, hate, blindness and anxiety give way to "the peace of God, which surpasses all understanding" (Phil. 4:7).

If you're not peaceful today, sign a treaty with Jesus. He'll pat you on the back with both hands.

8

The Blind Mind

Do you remember the words to the old nursery rhyme, "Three Blind Mice"?

Three blind mice. Three blind mice.
See how they run. See how they run.
They all ran after the farmer's wife.
She cut off their tails
   with a carving knife.
Did you ever see such a sight
   in your life, as
Three blind mice. Three blind mice.

Did you ever stop to ask why the mice ran after the farmer's wife if they were blind? I never could understand that one. I guess that's what happens when we lose sight of what we're doing. We go running off in all directions, sometimes the wrong direction, with disastrous results.

The opposite can happen, however. Those without eyesight compensate for this apparent deficiency with an increased awareness of themselves. One of my friends who is blind has an incredible talent for singing, writing, and performing songs, and perceiving the world around him.

On the other hand, an unusual malady of the eyes commonly afflicts believers who are unwilling to accept that God can work in their lives (or anybody else's for that matter) differently from the way they've always understood Him to work. It's the disease of the Blind Mind.

I call it Blind Mind and not Closed Mind because the Closed Mind knows it's closed and wants to stay that way. It's not opening the store for anyone. On the other hand, the Blind Mind doesn't necessarily know it's closed, which is worse. When afflicted with this disease, we actually think we are open for business, or at least, that's what our sign says. But the people who keep coming to our door can't get in. If people knew we were closed, they'd at least know to come back later.

Also, this disease is highly contagious. Just hang around others with a similar mindset, and soon, there will be a lot of sick people in one area: a church, a seminary, or some other assembly of believers who have been exposed. When we really don't want to hear the truth about the things we are closed to, we really can't see. Unable to deal honestly with the facts before us, we begin to lose sight of the obvious ways in which God is actually working in our midst. This is the most noticeable symptom of the Blind Mind disease—an inability to see something which is clearly obvious to everyone else. Simply, it's a refusal to see, not an inability to see.

The Blind Mind isolates us from other members of the body of Christ so that our perception of God becomes limited. Believers believe best when we have other believers with whom we can pray and plan. We may get a difference of opinion on a possible direction, but we may also get a different vision which could expand ours.

God may speak to us through another form

of worship or teaching, or simply just another representative of the Body. But we have to put ourselves in those positions at times to allow that to happen, understanding that God wants to use the full breadth and width and scope of the body of Christ in our lives. To be useful, minds must be stretched, not kept stagnant. If we have blind minds, we live motivated by fear and pride, and thus we quench the Spirit and prevent God from speaking to us.

Part of the Church's biggest problem today is that we don't understand how to make a difference in our world. We grasp for individuality instead of unity. This undermines the basic Christian premise that there is strength in diversity and that understanding this will lead to relationships with others with different perspectives. It's harder to fool ourselves when we are confronted by those who look at things differently and challenge us to get treatment for our myopia so that our vision can have a broader perspective. A whole new world awaits those of us who would renounce our Blind Minds.

The Blind Mind also inhibits understanding how faith must relate to others within the body of Christ in order to reach the outside world. In the early church, the believers worked together in such a way so as to convince the world that God was real. Jesus said that people would recognize His followers, however diverse and distinct, by their love for each other. Without this interaction between people who would not have ordinarily shared their lives, there was nothing exceptional about Christians and they would not have had anything to show the world. It's still true today. We will never be effective in outreach if we haven't first reached inside.

Not only do we inhibit God's working through us if we have blind minds, but we waste a lot of our own time trying to avoid the work. The Blind Mind responds to God similarly to the way Jonah responded to God: We try to run from God's work and need small reminders to straighten out our course!

The Blind Mind often differs from Jonah, however, in that we will pursue something but hardly ever find what we're after. We may pretend to seek more of God, yet we do the very thing that keeps God from speaking to us. We won't fellowship with those whose theology or worship or cultural experience is slightly different. We want to remain untainted from those points of view, sort of like the religious leaders who wouldn't get near a sinner or leper for fear of becoming unclean.

Instead of getting on a ship to flee as Jonah did, we flee God's voice and work by seeking to reinforce our position with more teaching on a given subject or by writing a book. In the process, we ignore the greater command to love our brothers and sisters. If we did that, we wouldn't have to write a book; we wouldn't be afraid of our differences.

Another symptom of the Blind Mind can freeze us in our spiritual journey. And we wind up doing nothing because our lives lack vision. I'm sure you're familiar with Proverbs 29:18, which says that without vision, people perish. As a Christian, I find that the greatest inhibitor to living for God is a lack of spiritual vision. We just can't see or believe that God could work through us. If we don't understand that God can work through us, then God can't work in us because we won't see anything to which we can commit. We're just like those three blind mice, running after the wrong things because we are blind to God's direction for our lives.

The best way to avoid the Blind Mind is to recognize the tendency of believers to surround ourselves with those who see things just like us. This only reinforces our affliction, rather than exposing it as a problem. We need to be involved with those who don't see things as we do, yet share the same love for God. We need to retrain our renewed minds to understand that diversity is more the model of the body of Christ than uniformity.

The apostle Paul continually confronted a world hostile to him and the gospel. That's what kept him going, though. It was through adversity and diversity that Christ empowered him. That made his faith all the more real. Non-believers have a way of challenging all we stand for, and rightly so. Christ challenges our thoughts and lifestyles so that we understand the commitment that needs to be made in order for true repentance to occur. Becoming a Christian is not like joining a club or a fraternity. It's not a change of address; it's a change of life. And part of that change is to relinquish our hold on our former lives so that we have new vision and new love.

The greatest preventative to a Blind Mind is to develop such a love for others who need to know Jesus that we look beyond everything and anything that is peripheral to our goal, and concentrate solely on meeting this need. We become so focused that we don't have time for the pettiness of the Blind Mind.

Love for others is an eye-opener. The best cure for the Blind Mind.

9

Golden Rules, Golden Calves

"Do unto others as you would have them do unto you" has been retired. The golden rule is no longer an acceptable dictum by which to live. Our society has put it on the shelf.

Instead, today's general consensus is to "Do unto others as would make you feel best." We seek to maximize personal pleasure and position and live by conquests rather than convictions. You'd think if someone could, they'd try a leverage buyout of God.

We've replaced golden rules with golden calves.

Much like Moses' experience at Mt. Sinai (Ex. 32), God's representatives in our society have remained too long on the mountaintop seeking Him, detached from and unaware of the unsettling situations in our camps. Left to their own design and without leadership by God's people, many in our society inevitably clamor for gods fashioned to fit their lifestyle. These craftsmen and artisans, modern day Aarons swayed by the voices of the masses, are the communicators, athletes, politicians, and businessmen of our day who have designed gold-plated gods of money, security, fame, power, and false religion. These become our golden calves, around which we revel and worship to our hearts' content. Not much has changed in three thousand years.

To the person worshiping a golden calf the only future is today. The Israelites did not want to wait any longer for Moses to come down the mountain with a word from God. They wanted to hear from God now. And if they couldn't hear from Him, they'd make their own god and put words in his mouth. We still do that—continuing to replace the one true God with new gods and new sets of principles to worship.

One such principle, the plunder attitude, tells us to strip the land of all its worth and then bow out. Today, the "lands" we plunder are not pagan civilizations, but our businesses, our governments, and even our relationships. The savings and loan industry has been scandalized, bureaucratic red tape and ego stymy most honest attempts at political reform as our leaders bow to lobbies and constituencies regardless of their own personal or moral convictions. Commitment in relationships is now equated with bondage because we've become so self-serving. We build only for ourselves and not for future generations. No wonder nothing has any value anymore.

In the plunder principle, we don't build bridges, we burn them so that no one can follow and make us accountable for our actions. Don't leave any evidence, we say. Burning the bridge also prevents *both* parties from getting back to each other. Reconciliation is thwarted and not considered important enough to invest the time, effort, hope, or honesty with another to reverse this trend. One look at our nation's tabloids will highlight that bridge burning has become a national pastime. The scene is getting increasingly rowdy around the golden calf.

This current climate is so unlike an attitude defined on a plaque which hung in the lobby of the School of Public Communication at Boston University: "Be ashamed to die until you've achieved some victory for humanity." It was written by Horace Mann, famous American educator of the early twentieth century.

During my four years of undergraduate work at Boston University, I saw that plaque each time I walked into the building. I couldn't escape it. No one could.

For my first two years there, I viewed those words as some corny cliché from the past. My reaction to it was a bit of warmed-over sarcasm. In 1968, sarcasm, idealism, skepticism, and cynicism punctuated the mindset of American youth. I was not much different.

But after two years, those words began to take on another meaning. They became important and convicting because I had become a Christian late in my sophomore year, and slowly my perspective on what gave meaning to life began to change. "Do unto others" became real, and establishing meaningful relationships based on Christ's love became important to me. Jesus' admonition to serve your fellow man was never left as optional.

Today, our culture tells us that those words by Horace Mann and the words of Jesus have little place in our lives. Regrettably, the words on the bumper sticker, "He who dies with the most toys wins," accurately communicates the material and spiritual mentality of our current age. Society seems to want to expunge all mention of God from its vocabulary to coincide with the plunder attitude and its extravagant pursuit of pleasure and self-gratification.

Unfortunately, some of this ideology has slipped into our redeemed minds. We serve only ourselves when we have no active involvement or concern in the actual caring ministry of the church. A self-serving Christianity is an oxymoron. In this case, we actually plunder our relationship with God.

We set up our own golden calf to dance around and feign worship when we, as a church, are so preoccupied with ourselves that we ignore the needs of others. We are content merely "to preach the gospel," using that as a whitewashed excuse to clothe the nakedness of our theology. If we won't do unto others what we would like to have done for ourselves, then we have set up an idol. It is impossible to "do unto others" unless we first have others at heart. Our American brand of Christianity wants a comfortable faith in the right surroundings instead of being comfortable with our faith regardless of our surroundings.

Jesus calls everyone to die to their desires in favor of a life of self-sacrifice and conscious devotion to Him. But, we don't like words like *die*. It's so foreign, so un-American. You certainly can't enjoy life and its pleasures when you're dead. If Christians aren't concerned enough that others might live, certainly the world is not going to take up His cross. It's much too heavy when we're carrying an armload of material pleasures. And our hands are already full.

Fortunately, there are those who want to serve others as the Christ of Matthew 25, by visiting those in prison, whether an actual prison with barbed wire or the prisons of poverty and homelessness, or by caring for the widow and orphan, or for that unwed mother overcome by uncertainty. The idea is to tangibly express Christ. In doing this, we achieve our victory for humanity.

So, Christian, ask yourself those words by Horace Mann. What will be your victory for humanity when you face the Lord? Will you be a restorer, nurturing the land and relationships God has given you? Or will you be a plunderer, interested only in the spoils of the land and burned bridges? Hopefully, your arms will not be loaded with things for yourself, but with people for God.

About the Author

Joseph Battaglia is Vice President of National Sales and Promotions for Communicom Corp. of America, which owns and operates contemporary Christian radio stations WWDJ, New York, WZZD, Philadelphia and KSLR, San Antonio. Prior to his current position, Battaglia was for eight years General Manager of WWDJ, which covers the New York Metropolitan area and is considered to be one of the largest and most influential Christian radio stations in the country.

This long-standing involvement with Christian radio has led him to an active involvement with gospel music. He has served on the board of the Gospel Music Association for ten years and has been chairman of the National Christian Radio Seminar for the past five years. He has been involved both independently and through WWDJ in numerous contemporary Christian music concerts, and has been the East Coast correspondent for *Contemporary Christian Music Magazine*, and continues to write freelance articles for publications such as *CCM*, *Religious Broad-*

casting Magazine, and *Christian Research Report.*

Battaglia grew up in New Jersey and went to Boston University for undergraduate work in communications. He received a B.S. in journalism, magna cum laude, from Boston University in 1972. After returning home to find a critical lack of channels for communicating Christian news and information in the metropolitan area, and sensing a calling from the Lord, he researched the need for such a communication vehicle and founded a publication for the New York Christian community, *Alternatives,* which was published for eight years.

He also serves on the board of the Walter Hoving Home, a Christ-centered rehabilitation home for troubled women, located in Garrison, New York, and The King's College in Briarcliff Manor, New York.

He currently resides in Wyckoff, New Jersey with his wife, LuAnn, and daughter, Alanna, and they attend Pascack Bible Church in Hillsdale, New Jersey.